FOR AGES 0 TO 3

Easy-to-play games

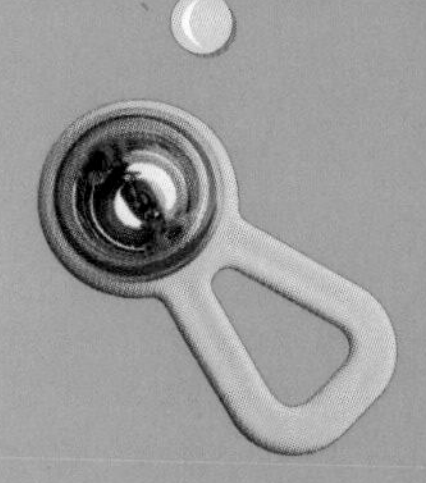

Supporting first learning

Stages of development

ALICE SHARP

CREDITS

British Library Cataloguing-in-Publication Data A catalogue record for this book is available from the British Library.

ISBN 0 439 98336 3

Author
Alice Sharp

Illustrator
Gaynor Berry

Editor
Sally Gray

Assistant Editor
Saveria Mezzana

Series Designer
Anna Oliwa

Designer
Anna Oliwa

Designed using Adobe Pagemaker

Published by Scholastic Ltd,
Villiers House,
Clarendon Avenue,
Leamington Spa,
Warwickshire CV32 5PR

Visit our website at www.scholastic.co.uk
Printed by Belmont Press

1 2 3 4 5 6 7 8 9 0   2 3 4 5 6 7 8 9 0 1

Acknowledgements:

The publishers gratefully acknowledge permission to reproduce the following copyright material:

© **Derek Cooknell:** p66

© **Corbis:** Cover, p7, p8, p9, p23, p51, p54, p60, p64, p79, p95, p96

© **Dr James Sharp:** p14, p16, p24, p26, p36, p46, p49, p52, p56, p59, p62, p67, p68, p70, p71, p72, p75, p77, p83, p84, p87, p88, p90, p105, p116, p119, p120, p124

© **Digital Stock:** p10, p23, p37, p38, p51, p52, p79, p80, p96, p111

© **Digital Vision Ltd:** p65, p80

© **Ingram Publishing:** p3, p4, p12, p15, p22, p26, p28, p31, p36, p41, p42, p43, p50, p63, p68, p72, p91, p93, p94, p113, p120

© **Photodisc:** p3, p4, p8, p10, p11, p16, p27, p32, p36, p37, p42, p47, p57, p71, p72, p89, p93, p94, p97, p98, p101, p112, p122

© **Howell, Dan/SODA:** p6, p11, p12, p28, p29, p40, p45, p63, p78, p92, p97, p109, p115

© **Powell, Dan/SODA:** p5, p22, p30, p65, p95, p99, p102, p106, p107, p108

© **Photodisc via SODA:** p35, p58, p101, p111, p112

© **Stockbyte:** Cover, p1, p3, p6, p7, p14, p20, p21, p22, p25, p27, p33, p35, p43, p45, p63, p74, p92, p97, p101, p115

Every effort has been made to trace copyright holders and the publishers apologise for any inadvertent omissions.

CONTENTS
CHAPTER 1
CHAPTER 2
CHAPTER 3
CHAPTER 4

CONTENTS
CHAPTER 5
CHAPTER 6
CHAPTER 7
CHAPTER 8

INTRODUCTION

Your baby's needs

In every new parent's voice you can hear the excitement and wonder as they tell you, 'It's a boy' or, 'It's a girl'. The safe arrival of your child is a magical and special experience and one that you can scarcely believe has happened. As you begin to realise that this new, unique and fragile being is here to stay, you will come to appreciate the enormity of the responsibility of caring for them. It is both an overwhelming and wonderful time.

Your new baby relies totally on you to ensure her well-being. The most important function of your 'new family' is to provide for your baby's every need. These needs include food, shelter, warmth, clothing, protection, security and above all friendship, support and love.

It is vital that your young baby feel the security of love offered by you or anyone else who takes the role of carer. Cuddling and physical closeness can offer this sense of love. The happiest moments in your new baby's world are those spent in the intimate bond of togetherness, with the people who love her. It is important that, as you build these close bonds, you talk to her and respond as she 'talks' back to you. Tickle her and whisper to her, repeat her name and yours. When she murmurs or giggles in response, then talk some more. Her early practice at listening and responding will encourage her to develop an understanding of the language and vocabulary that she will soon be expected to master.

These intimate moments are precious and, of course, not kept exclusively for a new baby. Toddlers and young children love quiet moments of togetherness and learn a lot from these enjoyable experiences. When sharing these intimate moments with your young child, it is important to create a warm, caring and quiet atmosphere that allows her to focus on you and the surroundings with which she is interacting.

INTRODUCTION

Stages of early learning

Your young child will learn in many ways and by using all her senses. Unlike adults who can express their curiosity, confusion and concerns verbally, the very young have yet to acquire language and have no experience to use in order to interpret their world. They are reliant on you to provide a meaningful construction around them, within which they can use all their senses to develop an understanding of their world and their place in it.

Toddlers become absorbed in using and understanding their senses. They are inquisitive and open to any appropriate challenges to explore and learn. They have limited understanding of how the world works, but are highly motivated to become active and to interact with their immediate and familiar environment. Your expanding role, and that of other carers, is not just to ensure that the needs of your baby or young child are met, but that you also ensure that her wants and interests are stimulated and challenged.

Within her third year, your young child will change dramatically. She will be extending and applying her new skills, interests and understanding of her world. The majority of children approaching the age of three have a sense of themselves as individuals and view themselves and their world in a very positive way. Children of this age also begin to consider others. They can feel a sense of duty to take care of and help a younger child.

Providing activities

One way that you (or another carer) can help your young child to develop is to provide a variety of activities. These activities should aim to cover a wide range of experiences in order to help her to learn and develop. The more you encourage her to think, talk and reflect on these experiences, the more she will remember and take away from an activity.

The games in this book will provide you with a variety of starting-points. Each game has a suggested age range, showing whether it will be appropriate for your child. The introductory section at the beginning of each chapter also gives lots of helpful information with regards to stages of development.

The entirety of your young child's experience – that is everything that she says, does, feels, sees, smells, touches, hears or tastes – can be used to create experiences for her. Remember that your baby or toddler is learning all the time, so try to offer high-quality, positive experiences. Every child should be actively involved in using their senses to explore and discover the world around them. With time, your child will begin to relate new experiences to previous learning and will learn how to share these experiences with other people.

Establishing situations which enable your child to make discoveries and to explore and experiment within her environment should be a regular consideration. Relationship-building with your young child is a slow but critical process, one which can be strongly supported by her interaction with her toys, you and her environment. It is important that you strive to make your child feel relaxed and happy in all these situations. This not only makes for an enjoyable experience for all concerned, but also gives your child the motivation to learn. Never worry about repeating popular activities. Each time a child is exposed to an experience, the learning that takes place may be different from the last time. Young children enjoy repeating experiences, not only because the activity is pleasurable, but also because it makes them feel secure and confident in their abilities.

While it is vital that young children be allowed to explore and develop skills independently from one another, it is also important that they learn how to interact with others. By mixing with other children they will begin to learn important social skills, such as turn-taking and sharing. These interactions will lead to a sense of self-worth and will improve their confidence. Although the activities suggested in this book have generally assumed a one-to-one interaction between adult and child, many may be performed with a small group of children or with one other child.

Learning through play

There is no doubt that babies, toddlers and young children learn through play. They progress in their play through various stages. Active participation – when they explore everyday items, new toys and a wide variety of interesting objects – should be based on sensory awareness. Through their exploration they will be introduced to the texture, look and feel of objects, and this is when they will begin to experiment with them. For example, if you pour a little cornflour on to a tray and let your child touch, taste, smell and look at it, she will gain an idea of what it is. Then, when you add water to the cornflour and your child mixes them together, a basic compound is made. She may then attempt to

make handprints in it, or perhaps to smear it on her hair, face and probably you! She is experimenting and gaining more knowledge of the substance. Young children learn from this type of investigation and involvement. They also learn from familiarity, and often the best activity is a repeated one, consolidating what your child has already learned – 'Let's do it again!'.

Once your child has been offered many opportunities to explore and experiment, she will progress to practising with the materials. She will use them in different ways for different purposes and through this practice she may imitate the world around her. For example, she may make a 'blob' from the cornflour and water and call it a 'tree', 'fish' or 'ball'. She is imitating her world with confidence. This confidence has developed as a result of the active involvement that has been a part of her young world. Having gained all this experience, she will move on to create her own range of masterpieces.

The adult's role

Adults are assumed to play a key role in the care and development of young children. The role of the adult is to provide the stimulus and materials and to invite the child to become involved and to interact. The adult should attempt to plant a 'seed' of an idea, then allow the child to lead using the resources. It is, of course, of great importance that the safety and security of your child be ensured.

Babies, toddlers and young children have no real concept of the vastness of their world. When you introduce your child to a new part of her world, you should make sure that she receives positive stimulation, feels comfortable and secure, and is given the chance to explore the world in her own terms. Attempt to offer an intimate, worthwhile and exciting range of fun-filled experiences to your young child. As well as meeting her essential needs, it is important to try to give her the best possible start on her road to individuality and independence.

Always remember that everything that you do with your young child should be fun. The purpose of this book is to help you to involve yourself and your child in a range of fun activities. Any learning that happens along the way is a bonus. Never set out to teach your child something explicitly. Be assured that if you present her with opportunities to play and develop, she will gain knowledge and understanding by simply taking part and enjoying herself.

CHAPTER 1

ALL BY MYSELF

From the moment they are born, babies are aware of their own physical needs for comfort and care. They know that their carers will make them feel safe, clean and warm. As they grow and develop, they begin to take an interest in the clothes that they wear and the objects that surround them. In this chapter you will find games and ideas to use during everyday dressing and personal care.

BONDING

New-born babies actively respond to their world through sensing noise, touch, smell, light and taste. They recognise their mothers' voices and those of other close adults. At this early age it is essential that you provide plenty of close physical contact to your child. When talking to him, maintain eye contact and wait for a response. Always try to talk to your baby face to face, bending to his level whenever possible. If he is lying on a mat, lie next to him; if he is sitting in a bouncy chair, sit opposite him on the floor (rather than hovering over him). While talking to him, maintain physical contact by gently touching him, cuddling or stroking his face or arms. This close contact will help to create a strong bond between you and your baby, as well as providing a feeling of comfort and security.

How you can help

- Be close to your child; whenever possible, position yourself at his level so that you can see each other.
- Use your voice to soothe or excite him, but remember that he will watch other visual signs of communication if he can see you, such as a smile, a wink or a frown.
- Always be enthusiastic when talking with your young child – he will enjoy your time together more readily.
- Be patient and offer your baby lots of time and attention. This will help you to get to know him and how he communicates.

BASIC ROUTINES

It is important, as far as possible, to establish routines in the early months of your baby's life. Eating, dressing, bathing and resting are all ideal times for strengthening intimate bonds and for establishing early routines. Naturally, you will always respond to your baby's needs as they arise, and enjoy the spontaneity which is all part of looking after a young child. However, the introduction of routines at an early stage is helpful for spending focused time together. Routines also encourage a sense of security in young children.

How you can help

- Always attempt to hold your baby while feeding and winding. Talk to him when you do this, offering praise and encouragement.
- Explain what you are doing as you carry out a routine such as stirring, filling a spoon or pouring the milk.
- Encourage your baby to feed himself when you feel he is ready, but do expect mess!
- When dressing your baby, tickle the part of his body about to be covered!

- Name the parts of his body and the garments that you are helping him to put on.
- Explain that he should wash his hands and face to keep clean.
- Talk through the routines.
- Offer praise for attempting even the smallest thing.
- Use little rhymes to involve your baby in the routines.

THE ENVIRONMENT

If possible, try to create stimulating environments for the areas where your usual caring routines are carried out. This will enable you to focus on the actual routine, while your baby is encouraged to participate in the activity itself. Very young children have a limited understanding of their surroundings and use all their senses to find out more about their environment. As a parent, try to feed theses senses. Using bright colours and patterns on wall hangings, mobiles and rugs around your baby's cot or changing station will provide visual stimulation for your young child. Play different types of music for him to listen and respond to.

How you can help

- Change the mobiles and pictures around your child every so often.
- Call his attention, not only to what is happening during the routine, but also to what he can see, hear and touch.
- When washing his hands or brushing his teeth, encourage him to touch the dry soap and dry bristles and to smell what he is using.
- After a bath, use large soft and warm towels to wrap him in. Call his attention to the touch of his pyjamas, blankets and teddies.

INDEPENDENCE

Within the first three years, if you have successfully bonded, your young child will become confident and eager to be independent. While you are constantly supporting and helping your child, it is easy to miss the signs that he is ready to try things for himself. Watch him closely and set little challenges. A good time to encourage independence is when your baby moves on to solids. Let him explore different tastes, smells and textures during snack and meal times. Children as young as six months will attempt to feed themselves and it is important to introduce finger foods as soon as your baby is ready. This will encourage him to feed himself. Inevitably, this will create more mess to clear up, but more importantly it will help in the development of key motor skills while your baby learns to manipulate his environment and objects in that environment.

How you can help

- Give your child push-and-pull toys for him to use.
- Offer support when required, but respect your child's independence and allow him to try to do as much for himself as possible.
- Invite him to gather some of the items needed for the routine to be carried out.
- Ask him to suggest what should happen next and act on his suggestion.
- Allow him to help with the preparation of the routine, occasionally letting him take charge.

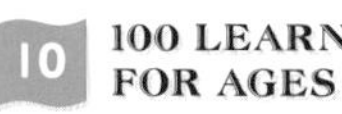

AGE RANGE
0–1 year

LEARNING OPPORTUNITIES
- To encourage active reaching and stretching
- To encourage purposeful play
- To develop a sense of curiosity and exploration.

YOU WILL NEED
Two baskets or bright boxes; selection of clean baby shoes, sandals, slippers, booties and socks.

THINK FIRST!
Do not let your baby suck or chew on the shoes.

My shoes, my socks

Sharing the game

- Sit on the floor beside your baby. Place the two baskets beside him. In one have a selection of his shoes, and in the second a selection of his socks.
- Let your baby play with them, pulling them and dropping them.
- Hang a sock on each of your ears. Bend down so that your baby can pull them off.
- Choose a shoe and tap it on the edge of the basket. Offer the shoe to your baby. He may try to copy your movement. If he manages to copy you, praise the noise that he makes. Offer him a sock to tap and exclaim at how quiet it is – 'Oh, it doesn't make a noise!'.

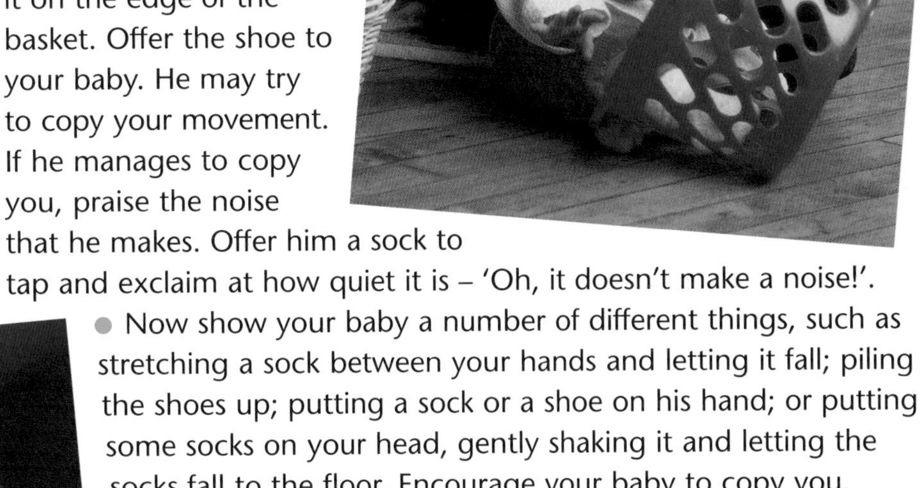

- Now show your baby a number of different things, such as stretching a sock between your hands and letting it fall; piling the shoes up; putting a sock or a shoe on his hand; or putting some socks on your head, gently shaking it and letting the socks fall to the floor. Encourage your baby to copy you.

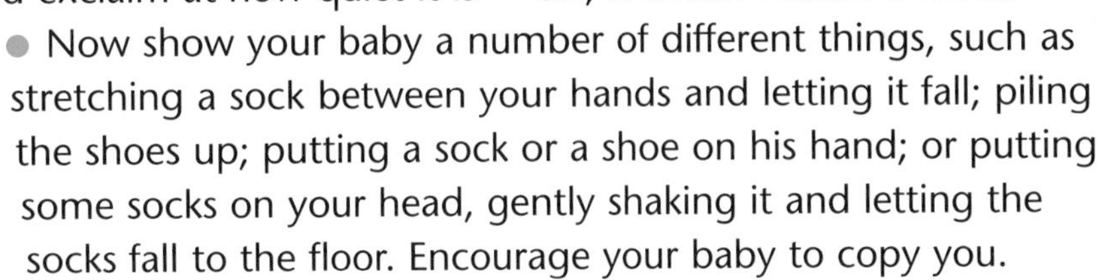

Taking it further

- Place two shoes on your hands and walk them along the floor in front of your baby.
- Hide a sock in each of the shoes and encourage your baby to take the socks out.
- Conceal items under the baskets and invite your baby to find them.

ALL BY MYSELF

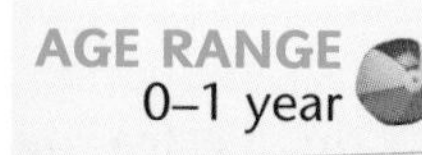

AGE RANGE
0–1 year

LEARNING OPPORTUNITIES
- To support recognition and awareness of self
- To develop social contact with a familiar adult
- To develop attention and concentration.

YOU WILL NEED
A quiet comfortable area; floor cushion; sitting pillow; large, full-length mirror (fixed in place if possible, if not, it must be positioned securely and care must be taken at all times).

Mirror, mirror

Sharing the game

- Sit your baby in front of the mirror and tuck yourself behind her. Look into the mirror together. Talk about your baby's face – 'Look at Amy's eyes'. As you speak, point to her eyes and gently stroke above them and beside them.
- Repeat with other features – 'What a little nose' (gently stroke her nose). Then repeat the words, this time covering the feature with your hand, 'What a little... (pause, and as you reveal the feature, state the name) nose!'
- Now draw her attention to her shoulders, tummy, chest and so on (depending on how long your baby is willing to sit!).

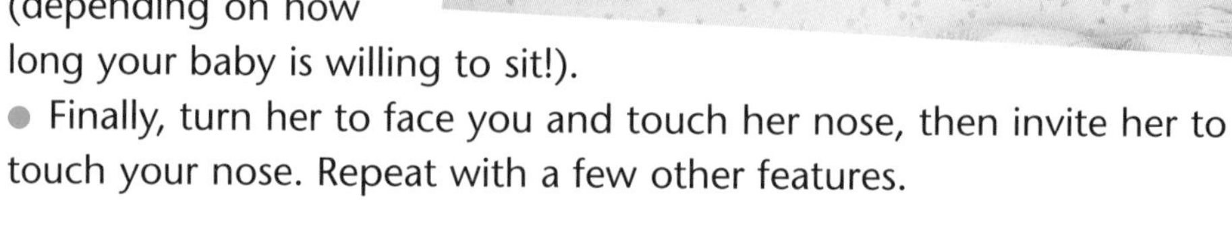

- Finally, turn her to face you and touch her nose, then invite her to touch your nose. Repeat with a few other features.

Taking it further

- Hold your hand up, move it towards the mirror and away again. Repeat with your feet. Ask your baby to help you to do the next hand and foot movements.
- Let her look at her teddy in front of her, behind her and so on. Each time, let her touch and stroke her teddy. Gently hide him and encourage her to look for him in the mirror.

ALL BY MYSELF

AGE RANGE
8–12 months

LEARNING OPPORTUNITIES
- To encourage enjoyment of manipulation of objects
- To support the exploration of objects in interesting ways
- To develop co-ordination of hand movements.

YOU WILL NEED
Three lengths of plastic pipe (attached to a wall if possible, if not, attached securely to a chair or table leg using sticky tape); basket with items that can fit through the pipes and a few that cannot. Make sure that your baby can easily reach the opening of the pipes, and attach these at angles that will encourage items to drop or roll through them and out the other end.

THINK FIRST!
Make sure that your baby cannot choke on any of the items that you intend to use.

Pipe race

Sharing the game

- Sit your baby beside the lengths of pipe. Offer him one of the items such as a ball or a soft toy.
- Encourage him to put it into one of the pipes, by pointing to the opening at one end. Alternatively, take an item and ask him to watch while you make it disappear. Exclaim when it appears at the other end!
- Repeat the activity as often as your baby wants to participate. Name each item that he chooses and count while he lifts it, making appropriate noises as the item travels and drops.

Taking it further

- Offer your baby a few items that do not fit in one pipe but do in another, and let him try them out. Encourage him to watch while you attempt to drop some items.
- Turn an old transparent plastic bottle into a pipe (ensuring any sharp edges are safely covered with tape). Encourage him to sit back and watch the item moving through the pipe.
- Join two sets of bottles together to make two long pipes. Send a ball through each pipe to see which one gets to the other end first!

AGE RANGE
0–1 year

LEARNING OPPORTUNITIES
- To develop more accurate finger control
- To encourage imitation
- To develop hand–eye co-ordination.

YOU WILL NEED
A baby stacking ring; mug tree; kitchen-roll holder; basket; plastic or wooden napkin rings.

Ring around

Sharing the game

- Place the rack on a low surface. Place the basket containing the rings beside it.
- Place a ring on the mug rack and continue to choose rings, placing them on the rack until your baby attempts to copy.
- Offer a ring to him and help him to place it on the rack. Continue with this until the rack is full. Repeat the game using the kitchen roll holder and baby stacking ring.

Taking it further

- On a long board (wooden, stiff card or plastic) place some hooks (fixed by tape or other method). Place a napkin ring on each hook and invite your baby to take them off. Encourage him to place them on again.
- Put a ring on each of your fingers and invite your baby to remove each ring. Next, place some rings on his fingers, if he wants you to do so, then let him take them off.
- Place some rings on your toes and repeat on your baby's toes if he likes it.

ALL BY MYSELF

AGE RANGE
1–2 years

LEARNING OPPORTUNITIES
- To develop fine motor skills
- To encourage hand–eye co-ordination
- To encourage listening to and following simple instructions.

YOU WILL NEED
A mug tree; small teddy; large teddy. On each teddy put a hat, scarf, some socks and a cloak (such as a piece of fabric fastened with Velcro).

Keep Teddy warm

Sharing the game

- Place the two teddies on the floor next to your toddler. Tell her that they have just come home from shopping (you are not expecting your child to understand, but you are encouraging her to listen).
- Invite her to undress the teddies. Demonstrate by beginning to remove an item of clothing from one teddy and then suggesting that she does the rest by offering her the teddy. Allow her to try and take off any items of clothing unaided, offering help when needed.

- When she has taken them off, ask her to tidy them away for later on the 'coat rack' (mug tree).
- Just as she finishes hanging the clothes up, pretend that Big Teddy has whispered to you that he would like his hat and wants her to help put it on.

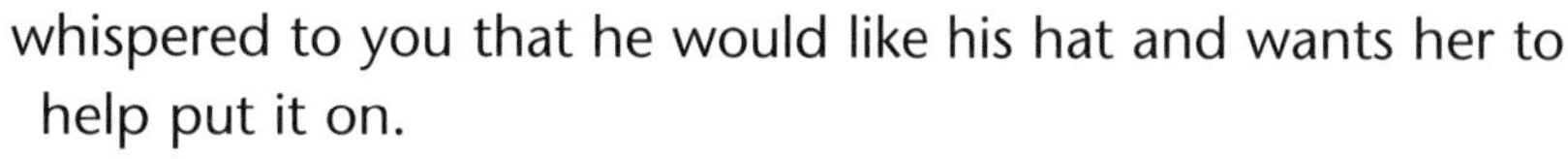

- Allow her to repeat the process for each item, suggesting each item and letting her find each one and dress the teddy.

Taking it further

- In a large box, place two hats, scarves, cloaks and shoes for you and your toddler.
- Tell your toddler that you feel cold and ask her to get you a hat, scarf and so on. Then invite her to put on each item too.

AGE RANGE
1–2 years

LEARNING OPPORTUNITIES
- To encourage enjoyment of using water
- To introduce the concept of floating and sinking
- To encourage investigation and exploration of materials.

YOU WILL NEED
A baby bath and two large bowls; water; apple; stone; sponge; feather; empty bottle; full bottle; ball; wooden brick; cup; twig; leaf.

THINK FIRST!
Never leave your toddler unattended near water, or in the bath alone.

Float and sink

Sharing the game

- Sit your toddler beside a low-sided baby bath, or if preferred, strip him down and sit him in the bath in some warm water.
- Hand him one of the items, name it and ask him to drop it into the water. As he drops it, exclaim, 'Oh, it floats!' or 'Oh, it sinks!'.
- Continue to hand your child each item, allowing him to look at it as you name it and then to drop it into the water. Repeat the activity until your toddler tires.

- Now take one of the bowls. Place it gently in the water and ask your toddler to put one of the items into it. Then encourage him to add another item, then another until it begins to sink.
- Place the other empty bowl in the water and gently lean on the sides of it, letting water trickle over the edges until it sinks. Talk about what is happening.
- Turn the bowls upside-down and balance some items on the underside, letting them roll off and float or sink. Encourage your toddler to copy you.

Taking it further

- Introduce bubbles and cleaning cloths, inviting your toddler to select the items he thinks can be washed.
- Drape a flannel over the items and invite your toddler to guess what is hiding underneath.

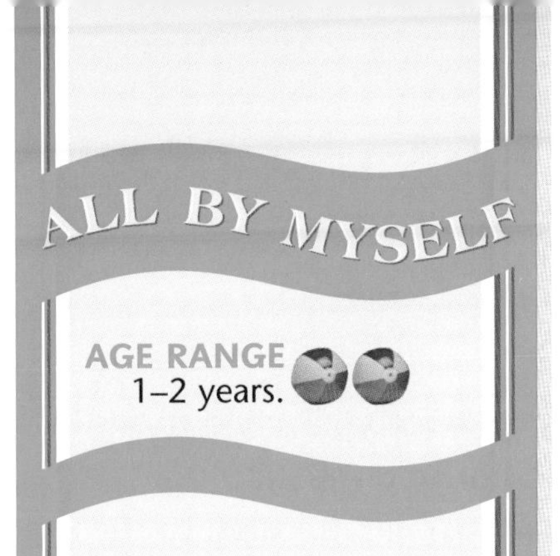

AGE RANGE
1–2 years.

LEARNING OPPORTUNITIES
- To develop visual recognition skills
- To encourage turn-taking
- To encourage use of everyday words and develop vocabulary.

YOU WILL NEED
Four A4-sized pictures or drawings of people in their underwear; cut-out card clothes, sized to fit the drawings (trousers, skirt, socks, shoes, hat, jacket, top, T-shirt or jumper – choose six items); large blank dice for you to stick on illustrations of the six chosen items.

Dressing up

Sharing the game

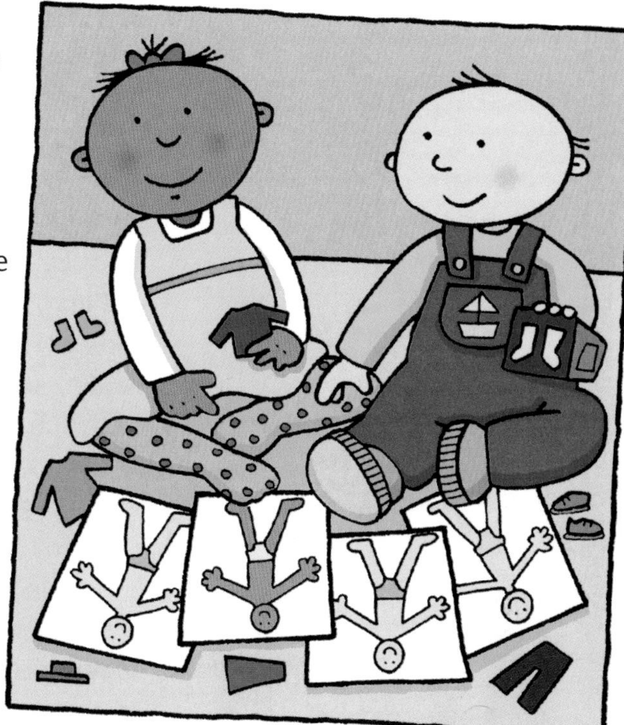

- Try playing this game with two children.
- Give each toddler a picture card. Talk about the picture together, such as the colour of the person's hair.
- Invite each child to point to the head and the ears. What can they put on these? Show them the hat card.
- Now ask them to point to their legs, then the legs on the picture cards. What can they put on these? Find the card showing the trousers or skirt.

Remember that you are encouraging the naming of the items and developing an association between body part and piece of clothing – it does not need to be correct.
- Show the children the dice, describing the illustrations to them. Invite one child to roll it and encourage both children to say what it shows. Repeat this a few times.
- Now hand the dice out to the children, encouraging them to take it in turns to throw the dice. Encourage each child to attempt to identify the piece of clothing, and help them to select and place the matching clothing picture on to their card person.

Taking it further

- Draw around your child on two large pieces of paper. Cut up one of the templates into different body parts and create a set of clothes by drawing on items such as a hat, gloves, a jumper, trousers, socks and shoes. Draw features and underwear on to the other template.
- Repeat the game with two children dressing the second template.

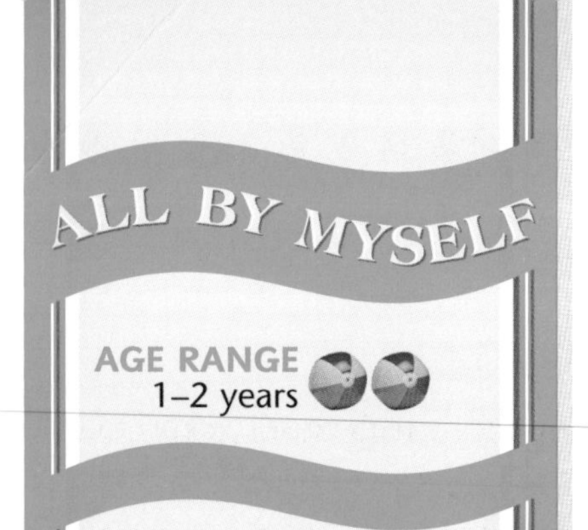

AGE RANGE
1–2 years

LEARNING OPPORTUNITIES
- To encourage independence
- To encourage interaction
- To develop an awareness of clothes.

YOU WILL NEED
Photographs or magazine pictures of children; change of clothes for your toddler (such as clean top, trousers and socks); adult clothes such as socks, T-shirt, jumper and shoes.

Clothes for me

Sharing the game

- Choose somewhere warm and comfortable for your child to sit, in her underwear. Sit her on the floor, beside or opposite you.
- Look at the photographs together, drawing her attention to the clothes that the children are wearing.
- Invite her to look at the clothes that you are wearing. Identify each item by name and touch it.
- Next, encourage her to look at what she is wearing. Again, ask her to name any item she can.
- Place the spare clothes on the floor beside her. Lift each item up in turn, describing it.
- Offer her one of your socks and encourage her to put it on, helping if necessary. Watch her reaction and respond accordingly. If she seems to notice that the sock is too big, then laugh and invite her to choose the correct sock. If she does not notice, then call her attention to how big it is, or try to put her own sock on.

- Repeat for the next sock, then try the T-shirt and so on. Ask leading questions such as, 'Are you ready to pull your sock on?' and so on. Each time make some simple jokes, such as attempting to put a leg in your jumper, or your hand in a sock and so on.

Taking it further

- Let your toddler help you put on your socks, shoes, jumper and coat.
- Encourage her to help you turn clothes back the right way and to fold items – all the while drawing her attention to the different items and where we put them on.

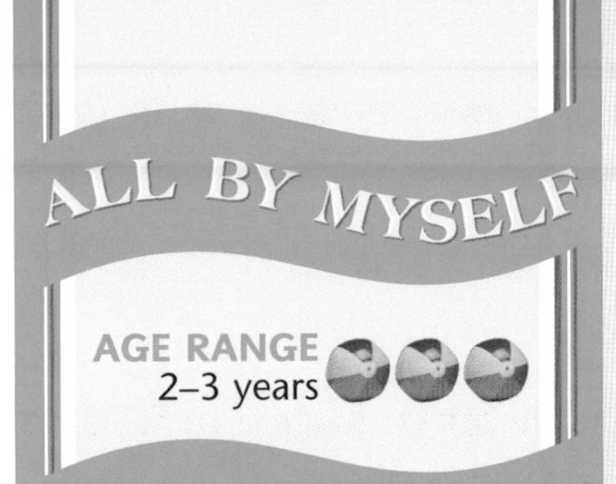

AGE RANGE
2–3 years

LEARNING OPPORTUNITIES
- To develop powers of observation
- To develop sorting and categorising skills
- To develop an awareness of different types of weather.

YOU WILL NEED
A bright box; children's clothes for different types of weather; four pictures reflecting weather, such as a beach scene, a garden in the rain, a park with trees (windy weather) and a snowy scene.

What will I wear today?

Sharing the game

- Look at the four pictures and talk about them together. Draw your child's attention to the weather that is illustrated.
- Look outside and talk about the weather. Ask your child what he thinks he should wear for the weather today.
- Now take the box of clothes and set your child some challenges. For example, invite him to choose some clothes suitable for a summer's day.
- Next, explain that you are going to select what you would like him to wear on a rainy day. Choose very inappropriate items. Challenge him to identify the correct clothes.
- Look at the pictures again. Ask your child to choose some clothes to match each of the four different weather pictures. Decide together whether any of these clothes could be worn for more than one type of weather. For example, a scarf is useful in windy and snowy weather, but not in sunny weather.

- Discuss what might happen if we wear the wrong kind of clothing for the weather. For example, ask your child to consider what might happen if we wore sandals in the rain!

Taking it further

- Suggest a set of clothes that are not appropriate to the day's weather to encourage your child's reasoning as to why they are wrong.
- Choose a few items and sprinkle them with water. Which items are wet? Are any not wet, despite the splashes?

AGE RANGE
2–3 years

LEARNING OPPORTUNITIES
- To develop self-esteem
- To develop an awareness of the need to care for herself
- To develop independence and personal hygiene.

YOU WILL NEED
Soap; running water (if not possible, small bowl of warm water); towel.

THINK FIRST!
Never leave your child unattended near water. Be aware of any allergies or sensitivities to soap. Children with eczema must learn how to cleanse their skin gently without rubbing.

Keeping clean

Sharing the game

- Explain to your child that you are going to show her a special way to wash her hands. Fill the sink or sit beside the bowl. Explain that while it is fun to play in water, sometimes there are also jobs to do.
- Put your hands into the water and rub water over them. Ask your child what else you need to clean them. If she does not suggest soap, then point to it.
- Use the soap to rub between your palms. Show your child how you wash your fingers, one at a time, using the opposite hand. Repeat for both hands. Submerge your hands and rub the soap off. While you are doing this, describe what you are doing or say a little rhyme, such as:

  Clean my hands,
  can you see?
  Oh, my fingers,
  one, two, three!
- Once you have demonstrated, encourage your child to do the same. Repeat the process yourself so that she can imitate your movements.

Taking it further

- Demonstrate, step by step, how your child should wet, soap, wash and rinse her face, remembering her neck.
- As you clean your child's teeth, talk about what you are doing – how much toothpaste is needed, how to make sure that all the teeth are carefully cleaned, and so on.

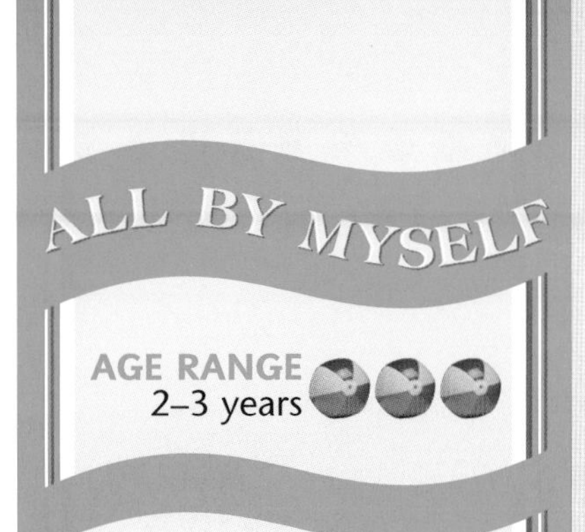

AGE RANGE
2–3 years

LEARNING OPPORTUNITIES

- To develop vocabulary
- To learn about features of the body
- To develop creative skills.

YOU WILL NEED

A mirror; old round cushion (or make a soft round shape to use); box containing a variety of fastenings, buttons and materials; needle (adult use); scissors.

THINK FIRST!
Make sure that you watch your child closely when he is handling small objects. Many toddlers have a tendency to put things in their mouths or noses!

Fasten it up

Sharing the game

- Sit with your child and look in the mirror. Point out the different features on his face. Challenge him to name some of them. Let him look at your face and again name the features that he can. Help him to identify any other features.
- Show him the cushion and box of fastenings. Encourage him to help you to create a face on the cushion and ask him to help by holding the items.
- Take the needle, stressing that only adults can use it and explaining why.
- Select a pretend eye (such as those used for dolls and teddies) from the box and invite your child to find the other. Glue a popper on to the back of each eye, asking him to hold the various pieces while you sew two other poppers on to the cushion for the eyes to attach to. When the eye poppers have dried, let him 'pop' them on.
- Glue a piece of felt to a piece of Velcro to use as a nose. Sew the opposite piece of Velcro to the 'face', where the nose will go. When the sewing is finished, invite your child to stick the nose on to the face.

- Attach a zip to the cushion (by gluing or sewing) to create a mouth.
- Choose a large button and ask your child to find a similar one. Invite him to look at his face in the mirror and ask him to think what the buttons could be used for (ears). Sew them on to the cushion.

Taking it further

- Continue to complete the face by adding wool hair, eyebrows and eyelashes.

ALL BY MYSELF

AGE RANGE
2–3 years

LEARNING OPPORTUNITIES
- To explore a variety of materials
- To learn about the purpose of objects
- To develop observation skills.

YOU WILL NEED
A box; variety of brushes, such as for hair, nails, teeth, shoes, paint, floor and make-up; photographs of children using the brushes.

What brush?

Sharing the game

- Put the brushes into the box and place the box in front of your child.
- Let her explore the brushes, encouraging her to suggest what each one is used for.
- Next, choose one brush at a time and ask her to name it and explain how it is used.
- Now tell her that you are going to play a guessing game together. Explain to her that you are going to pretend to use a brush and ask her to either tell you which one you are 'using' or give you the right brush.
- Look at the photographs together. Encourage her to find the brush shown in each of the photos.

Taking it further

- Ask your child to pretend to use one of the brushes. Explain that you will try to guess which one she is using.
- Invite her to move around the room or house to find other brushes. Add them to your collection of brushes.
- Encourage her to match two hairbrushes, two paintbrushes and so on.

CHAPTER 2

In the first three years of life children's physical abilities develop rapidly. Indeed, in the first twelve to eighteen months of life, most children grow from being completely dependent for all their physical care, to being able to feed themselves, to stand and to walk. Being lively and energetic comes naturally to children. The ideas and games in this chapter have been written to harness that natural tendency in a fun and stimulating way, helping to extend your child's physical abilities and skills.

LIVELY TIMES

LOCOMOTION

It is naturally a very proud moment for any parent when their baby takes her first step. Culturally we may see this as the first major milestone in a child's life after birth. This first step doesn't happen spontaneously or overnight – there are many minor milestones that your baby will reach before achieving fully independent locomotion, and these can be of equal delight for the watchful parent. In the first few months you will notice the automatic movements with which your baby is born, such as turning her head towards the finger that touched her cheek, the grasping and suckling responses, and kicking her legs and waving her arms in the air. Very quickly, perhaps by the third month, she will attempt to hold her head up when lying on her tummy or back, while kicking her legs vigorously. Once she has head control and her muscles and spine

are strong enough, your baby will be able to sit unaided. She may then begin rolling, bottom-shuffling, crawling forwards or backwards. By around her eighth month, she may become more adventurous with balancing and may attempt to pull herself up to a standing position. By her first birthday, like many (though not all) children, she will be moving around using support and showing signs that, with a little more confidence, she will take that first step and begin walking.

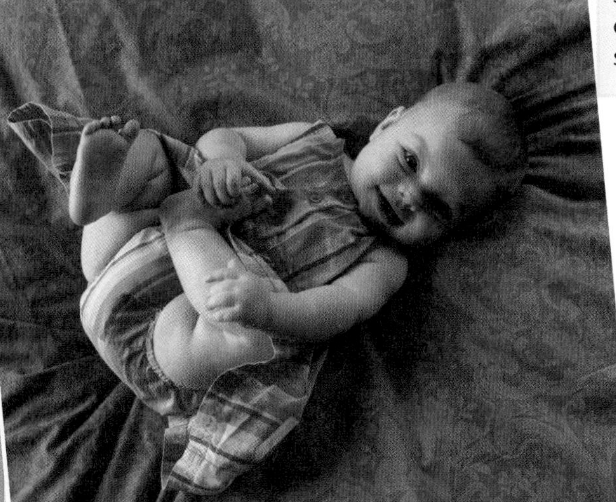

How you can help

- Give your young child lots of space to move around in – whether to roll, crawl or toddle.
- Encourage her to swing her arms and kick her legs by placing interesting objects near her, so that she can attempt to touch them.
- Lie on the floor with her, crawl with and generally copy what she wants to do, occasionally encouraging her (by demonstration) to try something new.

- Walk her on your toes, holding her firmly under the arms or by the hand.
- Help promote co-ordination and balance by introducing climbing frames, slides and trikes.

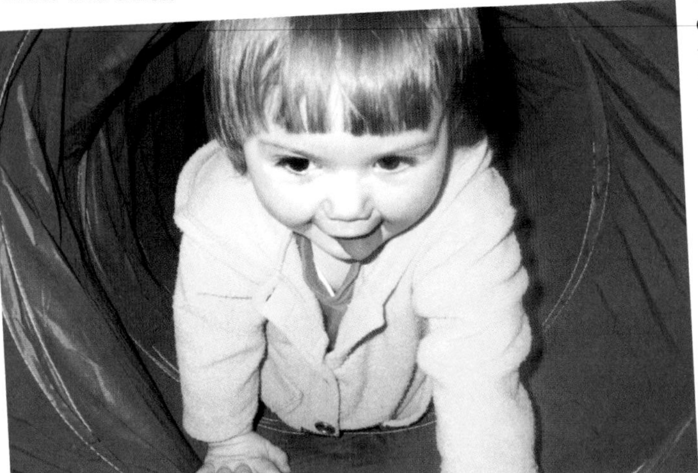

REACHING AND STRETCHING

Your child is unique and will grow and develop at her own pace – you can't force these events. However, in order to help your child reach these important milestones, you can watch her carefully and react positively to what you see. If, for example, she is reaching and stretching, make sure that she has ample space. Lie on the floor beside her and encourage her to reach out to you or a toy that you have placed on the floor for her. Set aside a time when you allow her to kick freely without the constraints of a nappy. Sit on the floor whenever possible, so that you can support her when she is sitting. Crawl beside her or bottom-shuffle with her to encourage and stimulate her.

How you can help

- Tie bright ribbons, scarves or materials above your baby to encourage stretching.
- Sit opposite your child. Play with something and make a noise with it, encouraging her to stretch out to you and the object.
- Place baskets and boxes of interesting natural objects beside her.
- Do some exercises with your toddler, such as jogging on the spot, touching your toes and so on.
- As your baby reaches specific stages of development, set up appropriate opportunities for her to practise and develop a skill. For example, if she is stretching, use mobiles, toys, pieces of food or any interesting object placed within or just outside her reach to challenge the use of this skill.

PHYSICAL WELL-BEING

Babies and toddlers are generally eager to participate in any lively experiences that are offered to them by their parents or carers. Children love the opportunity to play and, while they may play a game with their own rules rather than yours, they seldom reject any chance to play. However, play and games can be more than just fun, they can also help your child's physical and mental development. The development of both fine and gross motor skills is very important in promoting physical well-being.

As you watch your baby grow and develop, you will notice that she acquires a wide range of physical skills. She will be able to grasp, pick up toys and manipulate them with more precision as she gets older – these kind of physical movements are known as fine motor skills. She will also demonstrate larger movements such as crawling, standing, walking, throwing and so on – known as gross motor skills. Activities which encourage the practise of co-ordination, balance and control will help your child to learn these skills – abilities which, by school age, will become automatic for her.

How you can help

- Use music to encourage response through dance, movement and singing.
- Establish opportunities for crawling, running, jumping and balancing.
- Introduce rolling, kicking, throwing and catching.
- Carry out art activities – cutting, sticking, painting and modelling help to develop fine motor skills.

AGE RANGE
0–1 year

LEARNING OPPORTUNITIES
- To develop gross motor skills
- To develop hand–eye co-ordination
- To visually stimulate and encourage a response.

YOU WILL NEED
Baby bouncer or swing; plastic balls; tinsel; silver foil; ribbon or chain; baby rattles.

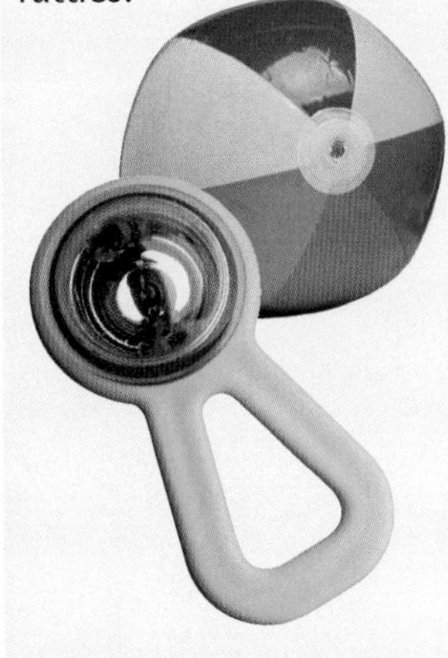

THINK FIRST!
Babies should always be supervised while in a baby bouncer or swing, and it is advised that they only spend short periods of time in them.

Bouncing treat

Sharing the game

- Sit your baby beside you on the floor with all the items in a small pile for her to explore.
- Take each item and attach it securely to a ribbon or chain.
- Hold one above her head and invite her to reach up for it. Tie it above her baby bouncer or swing as she watches. Explain what you are doing.
- Repeat this with each item until you have a variety of colours and sounds.
- Now invite your baby to go into the swing or bouncer, drawing her attention to the items as you lift her and secure her in the swing or bouncer.
- Encourage your baby to explore the items on her own by stretching to reach them, then shaking them.
- Place some more items on the floor beside her feet to encourage her to bounce and nudge them.

Taking it further

- On each side of the swing, hang matching items, for example, a bell, bow and tinsel on each side. Draw your baby's attention to the bell and ask her to find another one. Repeat with each of the other items.
- Make up a similar game by placing an item on the swing and a matching item on the floor. Draw your baby's attention to the one on the swing, then point out the matching one on the floor, and ask her to nudge the one on the floor.

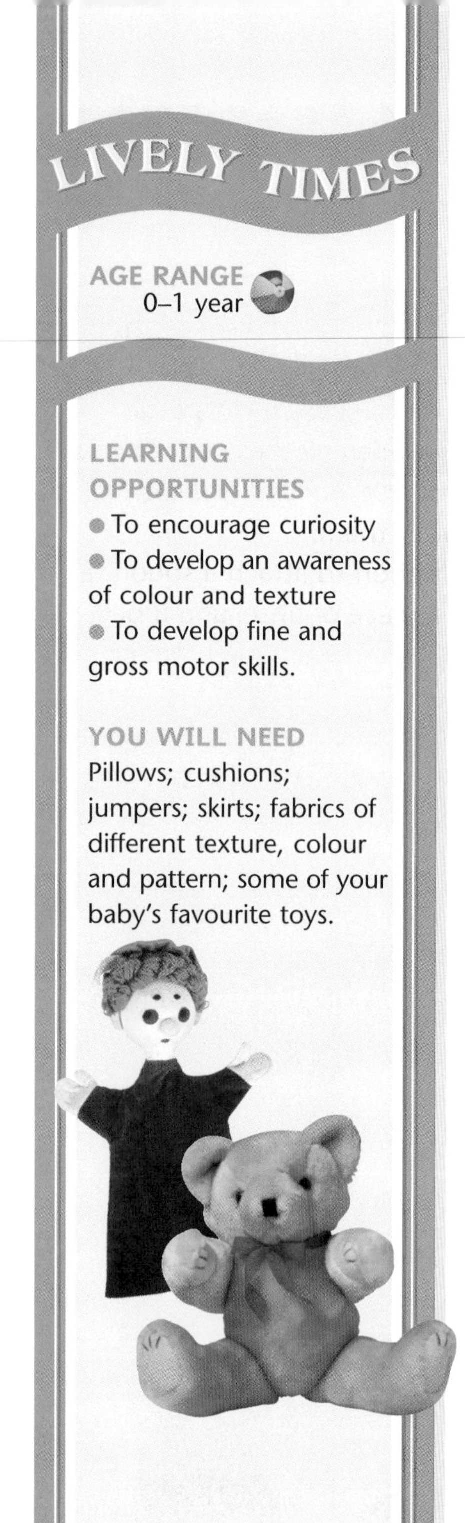

LIVELY TIMES

AGE RANGE
0–1 year

LEARNING OPPORTUNITIES

- To encourage curiosity
- To develop an awareness of colour and texture
- To develop fine and gross motor skills.

YOU WILL NEED

Pillows; cushions; jumpers; skirts; fabrics of different texture, colour and pattern; some of your baby's favourite toys.

THINK FIRST!
Never leave your baby alone with cushions, pillows and fabric, for risk of suffocation.

Cushion capers

Sharing the game

- Gather the pillows and cushions beside your baby and let him watch while you cover them with the material.
- Wrap the fabrics and clothing around some of the cushions. Put out one or two for your baby to lie on and crawl over.
- Add one or two cushions every few minutes. Try hiding behind some to play 'Peek-a-boo'.
- Encourage your baby to explore the 'mountain' of textures. Show him the different patterns and colours.
- Match the colour of a toy to a pillow. Hide the toy underneath the pillow and encourage your baby to find it again.

Taking it further

- Fill some of the cushions with beans or crinkly paper to create interesting textures.
- Securely attach some bows, bells, beads and buttons to the edges of the cushions. Watch your baby carefully when he is handling these accessories and never leave him alone with them.
- Select a few pillowcases, open them and hide some toys underneath or inside them for your baby to try to find. Help him with any zips or buttons.

AGE RANGE
0–1 year

LEARNING OPPORTUNITIES
- To encourage exploration of unfamiliar items
- To encourage manipulation of weight from sitting to standing
- To provide experience of the world at different levels.

YOU WILL NEED
Three curtain poles (one wooden, one metal, one plastic); variety of wooden, metal and plastic objects that can be attached securely; ribbons (silver, coloured and natural) to attach the objects.

THINK FIRST!
Make sure that the poles are positioned firmly and the items secured carefully.

Hang it up

Sharing the game

- Safely secure the three curtain poles – one at your baby's eye level when sitting, one at her eye level when standing and one above head height to encourage stretching. Sit your baby beside the poles.
- Use natural-coloured ribbon to tie a wooden clothes peg, a small twig, a fir cone, a loofah and a sponge to the wooden pole. Let your baby sit in front of the items and play with them.
- On the higher, metal pole, use silver ribbon to attach a spoon, a twist of silver foil, a strong silver chain, a piece of tinsel and a bell. Draw your baby's attention to these items and encourage her to stretch up and tap each one.
- On the third, plastic pole, attach some plastic items with brightly-coloured ribbons. Encourage your baby to pull herself to standing. Stay close by, particularly if she is unsteady. Help her to explore the hanging items.

Taking it further

- Swap the ribbons on the high pole for elastic, so that your baby can stretch and gently ping the items on the poles. Ensure that the items are high enough so that they do not rebound and hurt your baby.
- Fill a basket with some of your baby's favourite toys and some laminated photographs. Invite your baby to select some of the items for you to hang on the poles.

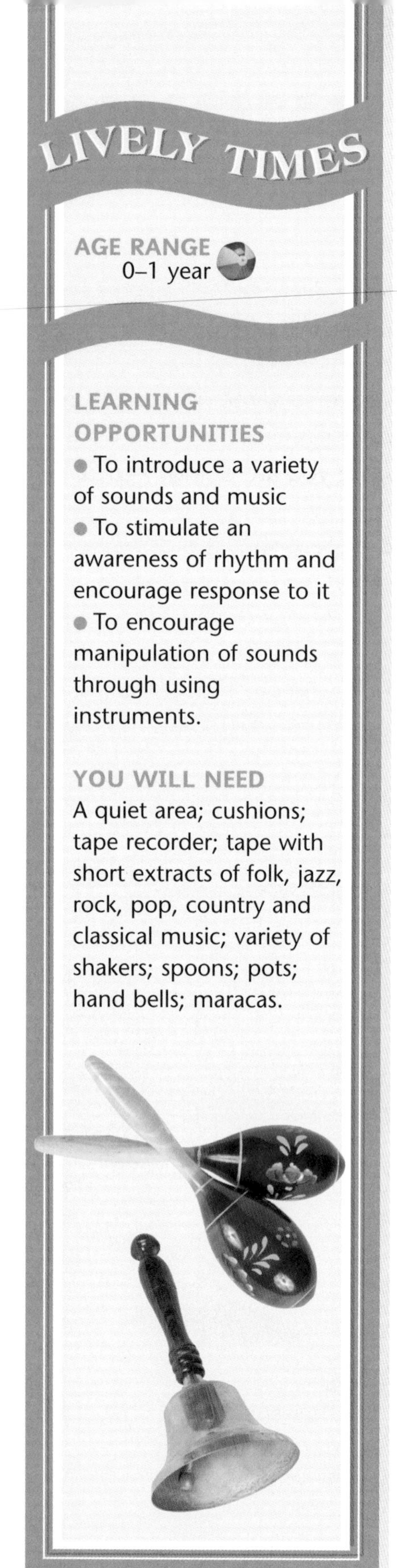

LIVELY TIMES

AGE RANGE
0–1 year

LEARNING OPPORTUNITIES
- To introduce a variety of sounds and music
- To stimulate an awareness of rhythm and encourage response to it
- To encourage manipulation of sounds through using instruments.

YOU WILL NEED
A quiet area; cushions; tape recorder; tape with short extracts of folk, jazz, rock, pop, country and classical music; variety of shakers; spoons; pots; hand bells; maracas.

Listen, hear

Sharing the game

- Sit with your baby in a quiet, dimly lit area, on cushions or a soft rug.
- Play the music that you have selected on your tape. Encourage your baby to listen carefully and respond to the music.
- Name each type of music so that you are using a little language.
- To start with, allow your baby to react and respond in his own way. Then, if appropriate, tap, shake, move or bounce yourself. Describe your movements as you respond to the music. Your baby may copy you or react in some way to your movements.
- Lie down beside your baby on the floor and ask him to lie down too. Tap your feet in time to the music. Then gently tap his cheeks, his nose and his chin in time to the music. Show him how music can be fun and stimulating.

Taking it further

- Offer props and instruments so that your baby can respond in a different way.
- Pick your baby up and bounce him on your knee, rocking from side to side. Lift him high, gently swing him or dance him around the room in time to the beat of the music.

AGE RANGE
1–2 years

LEARNING OPPORTUNITIES
- To develop an awareness of how the body moves
- To develop gross motor skills through exercise
- To encourage an awareness of action and consequence (for example, 'if I stretch I can reach something that I would like').

YOU WILL NEED
A clear floor space; some cut-out cartoon characters; postcards or photographs.

Exercise, exercise

Sharing the game

- Cover the photographs or postcards with clear sticky-backed plastic and place them around your space. You may like to tape some of them to the floor.
- Sit on the floor opposite your toddler, near to some of the pictures.
- Now make some movements with your arms. Start by leaning forwards to touch the floor. Talk about what you are doing. Repeat the movement with your other arm.
- Next, lift one of your arms straight up. Repeat with the other arm. Encourage your child to copy when she is ready, but never force her.
- Stretch up high with both arms. Explain what you are doing, even if you feel that your baby does not understand.
- Now encourage her to stretch to reach the pictures that are placed around the floor. Position and reposition the pictures to encourage your child to bend and stretch from sitting, kneeling, lying and standing positions.

Taking it further

- With your baby in a sitting position, play some catching and throwing games. Encourage her to reach towards you to catch something.
- Sit just out of reach with a ball, a bell or other such toys.
- Challenge your toddler to stand beside a specified picture (for example, that of a zebra) and ask her to walk to another specified picture (for example, that of a bear).

LEARNING OPPORTUNITIES

- To introduce the idea of using muscles to move objects
- To develop hand–eye co-ordination
- To discover how to manipulate objects.

YOU WILL NEED

A large box or bin; paints; tissue, crêpe and coloured paper; glue; selection of small items such as a variety of balls, beanbag, pompom and used cotton reels.

Ready, aim, go

Sharing the game

- Sit with your toddler and invite him to help you to decorate the box or bin. Paint it or use glue to stick on bright pieces of tissue, crêpe and coloured paper.
- Place the small items beside the decorated box.
- Invite your toddler to hold an item above the opening and wait until you say, 'Go!' to drop it inside.
- Repeat this a few times, introducing the words 'ready' as your toddler picks an item up, 'aim' as he positions it above, and 'go' as he drops it.
- Now put the box or bin on its side and sit with your toddler in front of the opening. Offer him a selection of balls to roll into the box. Use the words 'ready, aim and go' again.
- Offer other items for your toddler to roll, moving further away to make it a little more challenging.

Taking it further

- Stand the box upright, move a little bit away from it and encourage your toddler to gently throw the items into the box.
- Decorate the box to make it look like a tiger, with a large mouth as the opening. Encourage your toddler to throw light objects, such as a piece of plastic fruit or a scrunched-up piece of tissue paper, into the tiger's mouth.

LIVELY TIMES

AGE RANGE
1–2 years

LEARNING OPPORTUNITIES
- To introduce new objects and stimulate curiosity
- To introduce new vocabulary
- To encourage the link between making sounds and creating music.

YOU WILL NEED
Old instruments, such as a guitar, recorder, flute, violin and drum; pictures or photographs of people playing the instruments; tape recorder; blank tape; tape of a piece of classical music.

Real music

Sharing the game

- Ask friends, neighbours and local bands or orchestras if they have any old or broken instruments, or whether they would be willing to lend you any instruments.
- Let your toddler experiment with the instruments. Stress that she must be gentle with them, as they are precious.
- Now show her photographs or magazine pictures of people playing the same or similar instruments. Talk about the pictures together, relating them to your child's experiences. Name the instruments and ask her to repeat the names to you.
- Encourage your toddler to experiment with the instruments again, allowing her to create different sounds with them.
- Sit quietly with your toddler and listen together to a piece of classical music. Describe some of the sounds that she is hearing using words such as 'soft', 'slow', 'fast' and so on.
- Make a recording of your toddler playing the instruments. Play the tape to her. Does she recognise the instruments?
- Play the tape again and encourage her to join in with an instrument while you play another.

Taking it further

- Show your toddler a video clip of an orchestra or from the movie *Fantasia* (Walt Disney).
- Play it a second time and encourage her to join in with one of the instruments.

LIVELY TIMES

AGE RANGE
1–2 years

LEARNING OPPORTUNITIES
- To encourage a sense of fun and nonsense!
- To develop pincer grip (thumb-to-finger movements)
- To encourage exploration.

YOU WILL NEED
Picture stickers.

Sticky fun

Sharing the game

- Gather a variety of stickers that your toddler can easily recognise.
- Find a comfortable place to sit with your toddler and sit with him at his level.
- Look at each of the stickers, name it, describe it and encourage your toddler to use vocabulary in response to it.
- Invite your toddler to close his eyes, or explain that you are going to turn away from him for a moment. Stick a few stickers on your arms and legs, hidden under your shirt sleeves and trouser legs!
- Ask your toddler to open his eyes, or turn back to face him. Slowly reveal one sticker, exclaiming, 'Oh, what is this? How did it get there?'.
- Invite your toddler to peel each sticker off, as you reveal it. Leave some stickers hidden and encourage him to find them.

Taking it further

- Prepare an area with a few toys on the floor and some stickers hidden underneath for your toddler to discover.
- Ask him to stick a sticker on your cheek, chin, arm and nose. It doesn't matter if he gets it wrong.
- Stick some stickers first on your knee, then on your toddler's knee. Give him a piece of paper and invite him to stick the stickers on to the paper when he is finished.

AGE RANGE
2–3 years

LEARNING OPPORTUNITIES
- To develop fine motor skills
- To encourage your child to treat objects and equipment appropriately
- To encourage manipulation of fragile objects and an awareness of the need to be gentle.

YOU WILL NEED
Five balloons; rice; water; sand; three small bells; elastic.

THINK FIRST!
Never leave your child unattended when playing with balloons, for risk of suffocation. Prepare your child for the possibility that the balloon may burst with a sudden loud noise.

Soft balloons

Sharing the game

- Before starting this game, stress how gentle your child should be. Explain what you are going to do and talk about what is happening at every stage in the game.
- Ask her to watch as you half blow up the balloons.
- Invite her to select a filling and then ask her to help you 'fill' the balloons with the filling that she has chosen. Repeat with each filling (four in all), and leave the last one empty.
- Before tying off each balloon, reflect with your child that she has helped you fill four of the balloons and left one empty. Remind her of the fillings used.
- Now explain that you must tie the balloons securely with elastic.
- Mix the balloons up and ask your child to identify the contents of each. Encourage her to remember what she has put in each, then to shake the balloons to check her guess.
- Invite your child to roll the balloons to you or to gently bounce them on the elastic.

Taking it further

- Challenge your child to identify what is inside each balloon (use a different colour or shape for each filling and make a note of what goes in each one, so that you can help her to guess). Remember that what is important is not that your child is getting it right, but that she is attempting to make a guess.

AGE RANGE
2–3 years

LEARNING OPPORTUNITIES
- To introduce the investigation of sound
- To develop concentration and listening skills
- To develop ability to make and identify sounds.

YOU WILL NEED
A box (decorated with musical notes); ten musical sound makers such as maracas, bells, wooden blocks and so on (sets of two each).

Musical match

Sharing the game

- Gather the sound makers and place them in the box.
- Let your child choose a sound maker. Name it for him and ask him to try to say the name too.
- Invite your child to find the matching sound maker and suggest that you play them together.
- Repeat the process for each pair of sound makers. Encourage your child to say the name of the instrument and ask him to describe the sound that it makes.
- Suggest that you both play each instrument, in turn, slowly, quickly, quietly and loudly.
- After playing each instrument, ask your child to place it carefully back into the box.
- Now ask your child to close his eyes. Choose a sound maker and make its sound (you may need to play it behind your back or under a table-top to make it more difficult for him to peek!), then encourage your child to find its partner. Repeat with each pair of sound makers.
- Now reverse roles and invite him to choose a sound maker and play it while you close your eyes.

Taking it further

- Suggest that you use the instruments while you march. Explain to your child that if you play slowly, you must march slowly; if you play quietly, you must march quietly, and so on.
- Tell your child that you are going to hide the instruments around the room. Invite him to explore the room, and when he finds each instrument ask him to shout out its name.
- Describe one of the sound makers to your child and invite him to guess which one it is, either by saying its name or by showing you the corresponding instrument.

AGE RANGE
2–3 years

LEARNING OPPORTUNITIES
- To develop balance and co-ordination
- To encourage expression of ideas and suggestions
- To encourage thinking before movement.

YOU WILL NEED
Two skipping ropes; two large hoops; two large balls; large space free from hazards.

Hop, skip and jump

Sharing the game

- Tell your child that you are going to use the equipment to create an obstacle course. Encourage her to watch carefully so that next time she can try to set the course up herself.
- Try out some different layouts and ideas. For example, encourage your child to walk along the lengths of rope, then hop and skip along them. At each end, place a hoop.

- Encourage your child to jump up and down in the hoop, then hop along the rope and finish by jumping into the second hoop.
- Bounce the ball in the hoop, then along the rope.
- After you have made a few suggestions for your child to try, let her spend some time experimenting with the equipment. Praise all her attempts and describe what she is doing.

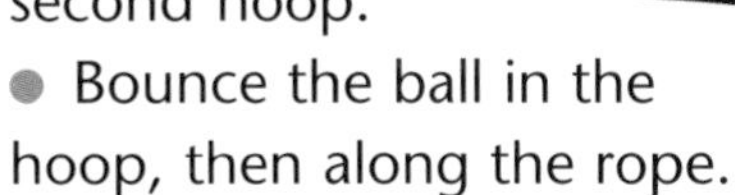

- Now set up the equipment differently, asking your child to make some suggestions.
- Remember that whether it goes smoothly or not is not important. The aim of the game is to introduce your child to using equipment and practising movements.

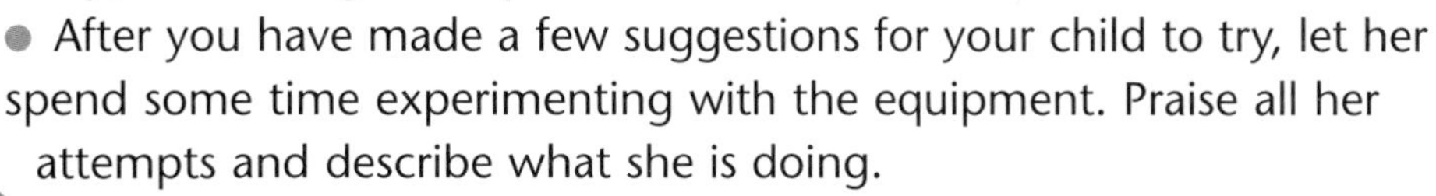

Taking it further

- Introduce some new ideas and equipment, such as beanbags, balancing on one leg for the count of three, rolling along the rope, lifting the hoops to crawl under, and so on.

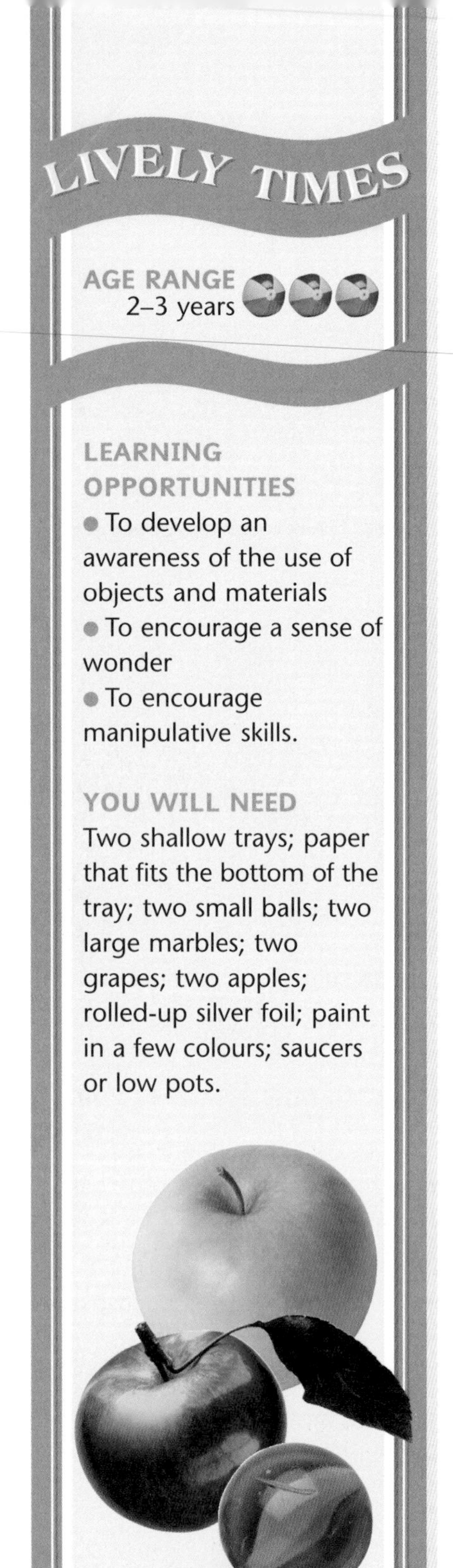

LIVELY TIMES

AGE RANGE
2–3 years

LEARNING OPPORTUNITIES
- To develop an awareness of the use of objects and materials
- To encourage a sense of wonder
- To encourage manipulative skills.

YOU WILL NEED
Two shallow trays; paper that fits the bottom of the tray; two small balls; two large marbles; two grapes; two apples; rolled-up silver foil; paint in a few colours; saucers or low pots.

Ball painting

Sharing the game

- Place all the items on a low table or a clear floor space.
- Ask your child what he thinks he could do with the items. Praise his suggestions and, if you have time, try some of the ideas out. Explain that you can try any other suggestions another time.
- Introduce the game by demonstration. Explain to your child that he can do the same as you with his tray and other items.

- Take the tray and place a piece of paper at the bottom. Pour three or more colours of paint into saucers or low pots.
- Choose one of the items, dip it into paint, then place it on the paper. Invite your child to pick something too. Gently tip the tray, rolling the item around, making trails across the paper. Encourage your child to do the same with his item, supporting him if needed.
- Repeat with other colours and items.

Taking it further

- Withdraw the tray and use lining paper for your child to roll the items over. Display as a wall hanging.
- Repeat this activity with an old sheet and special fabric paints instead. Help your child to make some new place mats, curtains, or a table-cloth for snack time.

CHAPTER 3

MEAL TIMES

Meal times with young children can be one of the most stressful parts of the day. Try approaching meal times in a relaxed and fun manner. You may find that helping your child to enjoy and focus on the food and the setting, as well as the smell, colour and texture of the food, will make for a less stressful experience. The games and ideas in this chapter will help you to achieve this goal!

SOCIALISATION

Eating is an ideal time to develop social skills. Providing opportunities for your toddler to be involved in the preparation and selection of what he will eat can encourage him to share and take turns. If you create situations that encourage him to participate, then he will look forward to the food and develop positive eating habits.

Young children enjoy company while they eat, learning from others how to behave with food. Once your toddler is keen to feed himself, do not worry about mess. Ensure that you use easy-to-wash-and-wipe utensils and that you have set aside enough time for your toddler to eat at the pace that he is comfortable with. It is important to listen when he indicates that he has had enough.

How you can help

- Gather two of each item (plates, spoons, cups and so on) and present them saying, 'One for baby, one for me'.
- Pour your baby's drink, then make a big issue of sharing the rest between all the people who are having a snack as well. Encourage him to say 'please' and 'thank you'.
- Invite your toddler to offer around a plate of crisps, fruit, biscuits or sandwiches, encouraging him to ask, 'Would you like one?'.
- Invite your child to join in the preparation, such as washing fruit or making sandwiches.
- Draw his attention to manners, encouraging him to use verbal communication whenever appropriate.

HEALTHY EATING

Positive eating habits can be encouraged early through healthy eating. By feeding your baby a healthy balanced diet, you will ensure that he is given the opportunity to enjoy all the nutrients needed to grow and develop a strong, well-formed body. Young children who eat a balanced diet are

example, infants under one year should not be offered honey).

Breakfast is thought to be the most important meal of the day and can provide a good source of vitamins, minerals and fibres. Whenever possible, attempt to sit down with your baby, acting as a good role model. Aim to have a calm, quiet and relaxed breakfast of fruit, milk, cereals and bread.

also more likely to have lots of energy, keep healthy and be active. Healthy eating can improve concentration as well as helping your child to fight infection through being well.

It is not necessary to spend hours planning and working out a balance of foods. If you offer a wide variety of foods, for example, milk, protein (fish, meat or cheese), vegetables, fruit and bread, on a daily basis, your child will eventually eat what his body needs. If you introduce healthy foods and he becomes used to them, it will be easy to continue offering healthy options as your child grows.

When your baby begins to appear hungry between feeds, this may be an indication that he is ready to begin trying solid food. This normally happens between four and six months (but generally not sooner – you should always take your health visitor or doctor's advice). Introduce these gradually and in small amounts, ensuring that your child still receives the recommended amount of milk for his age. By his first birthday he will be enjoying a wide range of healthy foods. Check government advice and refer to your health visitor for the types of foods to introduce and for those to avoid (for

How you can help

- Always wash or wipe both your hands and your child's before eating.
- Talk about the food on the plate – describe it by smell, colour and texture.
- If introducing something new, encourage him to explore it by smelling it, touching it, then tasting it.
- Use positive vocabulary to encourage appreciation of healthy foods.
- Present a little of everything, or slightly more of the healthy option. Never overload the plate, as it may put your child off.
- If he is not keen to eat, suggest that you try the food yourself. Describe how nice it is, then invite him to try a little.
- Never force your child to eat anything – remember, he will eat when he is hungry.

TIME TO RELAX

Always attempt to make snack and meal times a happy experience. If you approach food and eating in a relaxed way, then you can enjoy this time with your child without fuss and stress. Meal times present opportunities for talking and listening to each other and are an ideal time to encourage good manners, self-help skills and independence.

How you can help

- Gather together everything you need before bringing your young child to the eating area.
- Sing while you place the items that you need on the tray or table.
- Talk to your child, explaining what is happening. It does not matter that he may not understand, but your voice will soothe and reassure him.

- Play some relaxing music.
- Invite your child to help with the setting out of snacks or meals.
- Make little pictures with the food on the plate.
- Use shape cutters for bread and slices of meat or cheese, to make it more interesting and inviting.
- Eat with your child, whenever possible, encouraging him to enjoy the experience by following your example.
- Serve food attractively and start with small portions, so that your child is not put off by too much food. Focus on the social aspect of eating. When possible, invite members of the family to sit together and create a happy and relaxed atmosphere.

AGE RANGE
0–1 year

LEARNING OPPORTUNITIES
- To develop pincer grip (finger-to-thumb movements)
- To develop hand–eye co-ordination
- To become aware of taste and texture.

YOU WILL NEED
One large bowl; four small bowls, or paper or plastic cups (such as cake cases); baby spoons; four different types of cereal suitable for babies.

THINK FIRST!
Make sure that your baby does not have any allergies to the foods that you select. For example, it is recommended not to introduce gluten products until babies are at least six months old, especially if your baby has eczema, or if there is a family history of allergies. Check with your health visitor or doctor if you are in any doubt.

Fill it up

Sharing the game

- Wash both your hands and your baby's.
- Sit your baby on the floor.
- Take one large bowl and place a small amount of the four different types of cereal inside.
- Encourage your baby to lift and look at the cereal. If he wants to eat some, offer it to him.
- Place the four smaller containers beside the large bowl.
- Take a sample of each type of cereal and sort the different types into the smaller containers. Do this several times.
- Invite your baby to copy your movements. Do not expect him to place and sort the cereal correctly. Trying is the best game!
- If he is not attempting to pick up the cereal himself, place one small piece in your palm and offer it to him.

Taking it further

- Introduce spoons. Take one spoon yourself and give one to your baby. Spoon a small amount of cereal from the large bowl into each of the small containers. Encourage your baby to copy you. If he is happier to watch, then continue to move the cereal yourself.
- Scatter the cereal on the floor or table-top and start to place it in all the containers.

AGE RANGE
0–1 year

LEARNING OPPORTUNITIES
- To develop manipulative skills
- To extend descriptive vocabulary
- To encourage the use of some of the senses.

YOU WILL NEED
Jelly in different flavours and colours; bowls; spoons; high chair or low table and chair with appropriate safety fastenings.

THINK FIRST!
Make sure that your baby is not allergic to any of the foods that you are using. Ensure that she will not choke an any small pieces of food. Only introduce lumps once she is capable of chewing.

Squeeze and stretch

Sharing the game

- Wash both your hands and your baby's.
- Sit your baby in the high chair with her tray in front of her, or at a low table.
- On the tray or table-top, place two or three flavours of jelly.
- Sit back and allow your baby to explore the jelly through touch, taste, sight and smell.
- Talk about the colours, using words to help her reflect on what she is doing, for example, 'Look, you are squeezing the red jelly!' or 'Oh, you are tasting the lime-green jelly!'.
- If your baby does not want to put her hands in the jelly, then offer her a spoon. Let her splash the jelly, spread it, spoon it and squeeze it.
- Make little piles of the jelly. Lift a spoon and let the jelly slide off the spoon on to your other hand. Talk to your baby about everything that you are doing.
- Encourage your baby to eat some of the jelly, now that she has enjoyed experiencing it with her other senses.

Taking it further

- Repeat the activity, but use custard instead of jelly. Add some cereal, raisins or small pieces of fruit. Encourage your baby to manipulate and explore the different textures and tastes.
- Put out bowls of custard and spoon it into a larger bowl. Invite your baby to try this too.

MEAL TIMES

AGE RANGE
10–12 months

LEARNING OPPORTUNITIES
- To encourage independent feeding
- To develop an awareness of the taste and textures of food.

YOU WILL NEED
A doll or teddy; three bowls; three spoons; copy of 'Goldilocks and the Three Bears' (Traditional); your chosen food; baby chair.

Spoon it

Sharing the game

- This activity is helpful when introducing solids and, later, independent feeding to your older baby.
- Read or tell the traditional story of 'Goldilocks and the Three Bears' to your baby.
- Invite him to help you feed his teddy. Sit Teddy in the baby chair and put a bib on him.
- Offer your baby a bowl and spoon and ask him to feed Teddy. You can carry out the mime for him to copy, if he is not confident to do so himself.

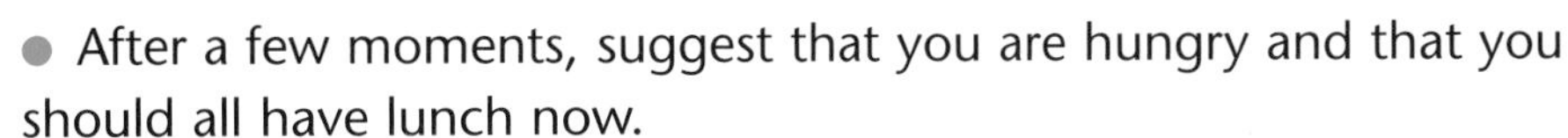

- After a few moments, suggest that you are hungry and that you should all have lunch now.
- Stirring the food in your bowl, encourage your baby to use his fingers or spoon (depending on his age and stage of the weaning process) to feed himself while you help Teddy.
- Offer Teddy some food and suggest that your baby should have some too. As he eats, praise the taste, saying, 'Mmm, yummy banana!' or 'Isn't this custard creamy?'. By praising the taste rather than the independent feeding, you will make your baby less self-conscious.

Taking it further

- As you introduce a wider variety of foods, use little rhymes such as:

  Stir, stir, one, two, three,
  Ready now to feed me.
  Stir, stir, eat it up;
  Food from a bowl,
  Drink from a cup!

AGE RANGE
1–2 years

LEARNING OPPORTUNITIES
- To encourage listening and responding to instructions and suggestions
- To develop listening and concentration skills
- To introduce the concept of pairs and matching.

YOU WILL NEED
Two oranges; two apples; two bananas; two grapes; one fruit bowl.

THINK FIRST!
Make sure that your child is not allergic to any of the foods used.

Fruit bowl

Sharing the game

- Sit with your toddler and show her the bowl of fruit.
- Name each fruit, offering one piece to her and keeping the matching fruit yourself.
- Ask your toddler to place her fruit back in the bowl.
- Hold up your pieces, one at a time, and name them. Invite your toddler to give you the matching fruit from the bowl.

- Now explain to her that you are going to hide one of each fruit around the room. Ask her to close her eyes (she will peep, but this will help!).
- When the four pieces of fruit have been hidden, hand her one of the remaining pieces and ask her to find the matching one. Offer clues and suggestions (it is likely that she will have seen where you put it!).
- Remember, the most important parts of the activity are listening and following instructions, and making attempts to match the fruit.

Taking it further

- Gather the fruit together and invite your toddler to hide a piece for you to find.
- Encourage her to help you to find and name the fruit.
- Try naming the fruit wrongly a couple of times, for example, 'Is it a banana?' when it is an apple. She may try to correct you!
- Make a fruit salad together. Invite your toddler to match the cut fruit with its uncut version.

AGE RANGE
1–2 years

LEARNING OPPORTUNITIES
- To develop an appreciation of food
- To introduce categorising skills
- To introduce new vocabulary.

YOU WILL NEED
Four food trays or bowls (of four different colours, if possible, or all white); foods of different colours (orange, yellow, red and green).

THINK FIRST!
Make sure that your child is not allergic to any of the foods used.

Snack colours

Sharing the game

- Place orange foods on the first tray and put it beside your toddler. Point to each item and name it. Invite your toddler to taste the food (ideas include carrots, beans, cheese and cheesy puffs).
- Place yellow items (such as a pineapple, banana, melon and maize sticks) on the second tray and repeat the process. Encourage your toddler to repeat the name of each item.
- On the third tray, place red items, such as tomatoes, strawberries, jelly beans and a red jelly cube. Repeat as above.
- On the fourth tray, place green items such as grapes, jelly babies and peas. Encourage your toddler to identify each food and express if he likes it or not. Ask him which are his favourites.

Taking it further

- On other occasions, put out some colour-sorted food trays at the same time. Encourage your toddler to notice the way that they have been sorted.
- Invite your toddler to select something juicy, something crunchy, something hard and something soft. Help him to sort the food in a simple but different way.

AGE RANGE
1–2 years

LEARNING OPPORTUNITIES
- To encourage sharing and turn-taking
- To introduce mixing and changing
- To encourage expressing likes and dislikes.

YOU WILL NEED
Three large bowls; one medium-sized bowl; five small bowls; wooden spoon; custard; instant dessert mix; yoghurt; raisins; apples; grapes; pineapple; biscuit crumbs; spoons.

THINK FIRST!
Make sure that your child is not allergic to any of the foods used. Read the ingredients of commercially-made foods, such as the instant dessert mix, to check for any additives that do not agree with your child. Be aware that toddlers may choke on small pieces of hard fruit such as apples.

Making pudding

Sharing the game

- On a low table, place three large bowls: one of custard, one of instant dessert mix and another of yoghurt.
- Tell your toddler what is in each bowl. Encourage her to point to her favourite, or to taste all foods and tell you which she liked the most.
- Then place small bowls of raisins, apple and pineapple pieces, grapes and biscuit crumbs on the table, again naming each item. Discuss what your toddler likes.
- Explain that she can make her very own pudding. Invite her to take a spoonful from one of the large bowls and put it into her own bowl.
- Then invite her to choose another item, spoon it and mix it. Limit her to two or three items, so as not to spoil the pudding.

Taking it further

- Invite your toddler to make the custard with you. Demonstrate how you measure out and let her mix it with you.
- Show your toddler how to prepare the fruit pieces and how to add them to the mixture. Make one large bowl of pudding to be spooned into a smaller bowl for each of you.

AGE RANGE
1–2 years

LEARNING OPPORTUNITIES
- To know that water is used for cleaning
- To encourage self-help skills
- To develop a sense of order.

YOU WILL NEED
A favourite snack; washing-up bowl or low-level sink; washing-up liquid; rubber gloves; wash cloth; washing-up brush; drying cloth.

Washing up

Sharing the game

- Put out a snack for your toddler and place all the items nearby. Ask your toddler if you need them for the snack.
- After eating the snack, ask your toddler to place his dirty dishes in the washing-up bowl. Invite him to help to wash and dry the dishes.
- Offer him the washing-up liquid to use, stressing that he only needs a little bit. Explain that you will pour in the hot water after he has poured in the cold water. Test the water with your own hand before inviting him to test it and declare that it is all right.

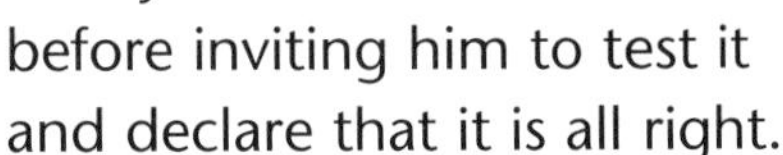

- Offer your toddler the rubber gloves, cloth and brush. Allow him to wash up until he tires of the game.
- Finally, give your toddler a clean drying cloth and encourage him to dry all the objects.

Taking it further

- Ask your toddler to clean the table-top or very dirty items such as mixing bowls or paint pots.
- Draw his attention to the importance of removing all the dirt and rinsing and drying when necessary.

AGE RANGE
1–2 years

LEARNING OPPORTUNITIES

- To encourage mark-making
- To inspire creativity
- To encourage manipulation of resources.

YOU WILL NEED

A4-sized card; sticky-backed plastic (or access to a laminating machine); selection of white, black and coloured paper in a variety of shapes and sizes; dishes of pencils, coloured pencils, white chalk, charcoal, pastels, crayons and felt-tipped pens.

Place-mat pieces

Sharing the game

- Let your toddler explore the materials. Talk about the colours together as she picks up something to show you.
- Offer your toddler a choice of paper.
- Choose a piece of black paper yourself and select a white mark-maker. Take the chalk or pastel 'for a walk' on the page.
- Repeat this with white paper and a black crayon or charcoal.
- Encourage your toddler to select a variety of mark-makers to create her 'picture'. Offer a different choice from time to time, in the hope that she will be tempted to use a variety of types or colours.

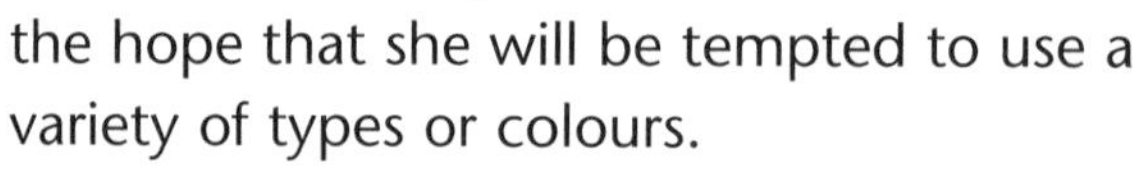

- Choose a few pictures from the selection that she has made. Mount a few of them on to a sheet of A4 card and laminate or cover with in sticky-backed plastic, to use as a place mat.
- Encourage your toddler to repeat the activity with a selection of other coloured papers and mark-makers. Contrasting or complimentary colours work well together.

Taking it further

- Show your child a selection of place mats and coasters, drawing her attention to the colours, shapes and pictures on them.
- Let your toddler use paint, glue, sticky paper and glitter to decorate paper shapes. Laminate them and use them as coasters or place mats.

AGE RANGE
2–3 years

LEARNING OPPORTUNITIES
- To encourage the use of vocabulary
- To develop an awareness of texture
- To develop an awareness of how food is made.

YOU WILL NEED
A variety of vegetables; large container for soil or a suitable outside area; soil; spoons; spades; knife (adult use); chopping board; savoury dips; water; scrubbing brush; drying cloth.

THINK FIRST!
Make sure that your child is not allergic to any of the foods used.

Vegetable fun

Sharing the game

- Before asking your child to join you, hide the vegetables in a container of soil or in the outside area.
- Invite your child to join you and to dig the soil with his hands, a spoon or a spade.
- As he finds the vegetables, ask him to name them, prompting him if he needs help. Ask him if he has tasted the vegetables before. Does he like them?
- Encourage him to tell you what should be done with them now.
- Together, wash each vegetable, encouraging your child to realise that he should 'clean' all the dirt off.
- Invite him to watch as you peel the vegetables.
- Then chop the vegetables. Involve your child by asking him to hold, pass and place the vegetables.
- Describe the inside, colour and texture of each vegetable.
- Suggest that you use the vegetables to eat the savoury dips.

Taking it further

- Invite your child to help you to make a vegetable soup. Chop some vegetables (such as swede, carrot and parsnip) and let him scoop them up and add them to the pot before cooking. Purée the cooked root vegetables and blend them with milk to make the required consistency. Add some seasoning and heat up the mixture. Eat the soup together for lunch.

Get ready for lunch

Sharing the game

- Look at the pictures together. Talk to your child about the way that the tables have been set.
- Now explain that you would like her to set her snack table nicely.
- Pack the table-cloth at the bottom of the crate or box, then fill it with the cutlery, crockery and other items.
- Give your child the crate and ask her to go about setting the table. Encourage her to work out the number of places to set, where to put things and so on. Prompt her when you feel it is appropriate. Make suggestions if it will help or when she asks for advice.
- If by the end of the activity she still has not put the cloth on, drape it over the table and settings, for fun, to highlight that there is an order to follow to set a table. Make sure that she still feels successful and praise her for her hard work.
- Repeat the process, ensuring that the cloth is placed down first. Each time something is placed, name it and ask what it is used for.

Taking it further

- Next time, allow your child to identify where all the items are kept in the house or nursery and invite her to gather them ready for setting the table.
- Provide sets of different-coloured objects, such as red, green and blue cups, plates and place mats. Encourage your child to colour-match the sets and lay colour-co-ordinated places at the table.

LEARNING OPPORTUNITIES

- To develop a sense of order
- To develop information gathering skills
- To respond to a stimulus.

YOU WILL NEED

Pictures, illustrations or photographs of tables set ready for a meal (from magazines); box or crate; plates; cutlery; cups; salt and pepper pots; napkins; place mats; coasters; table-cloth; low table.

AGE RANGE
2–3 years

LEARNING OPPORTUNITIES
- To develop pouring skills
- To develop the sense of taste
- To encourage manners.

YOU WILL NEED
Diluted juice (sugar-, colouring- and additive-free) in the following flavours: lime, orange, blackcurrant and strawberry; small transparent plastic cups; four jugs (transparent if possible); water in bottles; low table.

THINK FIRST!
Make sure that your child is not allergic to any of the foods used. Citrus fruit can sometimes cause a reaction in allergy-prone children (for example, they can worsen the symptoms of eczema). Use plastic bottles, cups and jugs for safety.

Making drinks

Sharing the game

- Sit at a low table with your child. Place the four bottles of juice in front of him, then invite him to guess what flavours they are by looking at the colours.
- Ask him to choose a bottle and invite him to pour some juice into a jug. Show him how to add the right amount of water and let him try it himself.
- Talk about the way that the juice and water mix. Ask your child to pour the mixed drink carefully into a cup for each of you. Help him if necessary.

- Encourage him to ask you, 'Would you like some?'. Show him how you reply with 'Yes, please' or 'No, thank you'.
- Repeat the process with a small amount of each type of juice, highlighting each part of the process.

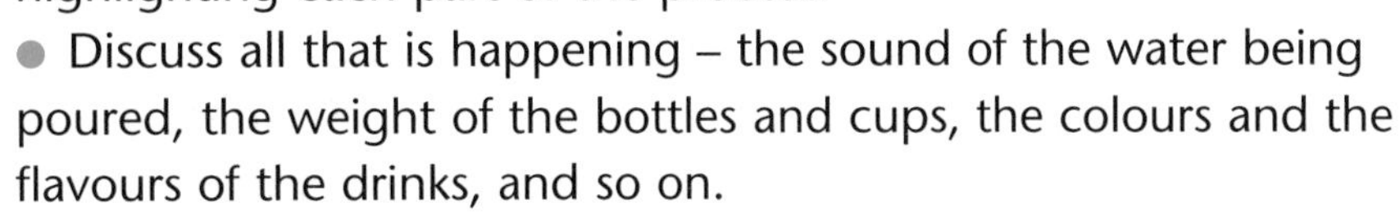

- Discuss all that is happening – the sound of the water being poured, the weight of the bottles and cups, the colours and the flavours of the drinks, and so on.

Taking it further

- Mix orange and lemon juice in the same way.
- Let your child watch as you squeeze a real orange and lemon. Invite him to taste the fresh juice, then the diluted juice. Which does he prefer?

MEAL TIMES

AGE RANGE
2–3 years

LEARNING OPPORTUNITIES
- To encourage the use of the senses to gather information
- To develop matching skills
- To identify objects.

YOU WILL NEED
A large bag or box with pictures of fruit and vegetables on the outside; selection of fruit and vegetables (two pieces of each); table.

Healthy choices

Sharing the game

- Place all the fruit and vegetables on a table and let your child explore them. Encourage her to touch, stroke, smell and look at each piece in turn.
- Then tell her that you will hide some of the fruit and vegetables inside the bag or box. Ask her to touch one item and try to guess what it is. Repeat the activity several times.
- Now place one piece of fruit in the bag and its pair on the table. Invite your child to put her hand in the bag and touch the fruit. Tell her not to take it out. Let her use both hands if it helps her. Hold up a possible matching fruit and ask, 'Do you think that it is the same as this one?'. Help her to consider whether it is round, soft and so on.
- If your child is ready to, encourage her to try to name or describe the fruit. If necessary, prompt her by letting her see the top of the fruit.

Taking it further

- Cut the fruit and make a fruit salad for pudding. Describe each piece as you wash and cut it together. Invite your child to try to describe one or two pieces of fruit herself. Enjoy the fruit salad together.

CHAPTER 4

Babies and toddlers have no concept of the vastness of their world. When you introduce your child to a new environment, try to ensure that she is stimulated in a positive way. This will help to make her feel more comfortable and secure and will enable her to adapt and explore any new part of her world. The games in this chapter provide a wealth of suggestions for helping your child to interact positively with the world around her.

OUT AND ABOUT

NEW HORIZONS

Young children enjoy exploring new horizons – finding 'treasures', objects and materials to experiment with. They love the independence that they acquire from the open space of a garden or park. When introducing her to a new place, allow your child the time to discover and explore. She will gain a great deal of knowledge by using her curiosity to gather information from these new surroundings.

How you can help

- Introduce your young child to different places – shops, the swimming-pool, cafés, museums and so on.
- When in a new place, describe what she is seeing.
- If you are using a new mode of transport, describe what is happening, what she can see and hear, but also what she can touch during this exciting new adventure!

Think first! Always stay close to your child – within each other's vision. Your child's safety must be your top priority.

VISUAL STIMULATION

When your baby is lying or sitting, it is a good idea to hang objects, interesting pictures and bright toys around to stimulate her. This can be done inside, but just as easily outside. For example, if she is lying on a mat on the grass, why not tie things to the bushes and trees or to the washing line? This will visually stimulate her and encourage her to reach out and catch the hanging items. As she gets older, she can toddle to these items and gather the 'treasures' herself. Hide items and objects under mats, on the grass, behind planters and rocks for her to discover and explore. This type of game will help to sharpen her powers of observation and she will have lots of fun, too!

Closely observe your young child as she explores the garden – digging in the soil, splashing in puddles or gathering ribbons from a tree. Ask meaningful questions and offer suggestions to extend her 'scientific discoveries'.

How you can help

- No matter where you and your baby find yourselves, there will be something to look at. For example, even if you are just waiting outside a shop, you can squat beside your baby or toddler and you can look in the window together. Show her something of interest, describe what you can see or challenge an older child to point out something that she likes. Always attempt to be at her eye level. This will ensure that you see things from her perspective, and not from a different angle.
- Decorate your baby's pram with photos, ribbons and a rattle so that she can look at them as she is pushed.
- If she is in a buggy, hand her 'treasures' from the path, such as twigs.

Think first! Make sure that your young child does not put small, sharp or dirty items into her mouth, for risk of choking.

EXPLORE AND DISCOVER

When out and about with your child, draw her attention to all that is around her. For example, speak about the changing weather, the clouds, the seasons and what she is wearing. When out walking, draw her attention to building sites, football matches, shop displays or squirrels scampering. When in the car, point out fire engines, blue cars, buildings – anything of interest! Whenever possible, maximise language opportunities.

Gather items to bring back with you – natural objects from the park, groceries from a shopping trip, or twigs from the garden. Allow your baby or toddler time to experiment with the materials that she has found. Try wrapping the items in brightly-coloured fabric or hiding them in boxes, and invite your child to discover them all over again!

How you can help

- Place items of interest near your child for her to experiment with.
- Hide items for her to find.
- Put a tent up for her to hide in and explore from.
- Give your child a basket to fill with her 'finds'.
- Offer her a viewfinder (make one by cutting out a small view hole in a large piece of cardboard). Invite her to describe what she sees through it.

FRESH AIR

If possible, allow your child to spend a little time outside each day. Sitting her in her pram in the garden, or walking around the garden or to a neighbour's is better than no fresh air at all. Always ensure that she does not overheat or become too cold and that she is properly protected from the sun. Spending time outdoors will benefit your child in a number of ways. For example, her appetite may improve, she will be more lively and energetic, and she may sleep more soundly.

Energetic play on climbing frames, bikes and trucks, and in tunnels, sand-pits and paddling pools will help to develop many skills. Your child's large muscles, balance and co-ordination will all be challenged during this type of activity.

Think first! Be aware that these activities, while being very beneficial, are often the cause of accidents. Whenever outdoors, keep a close eye on what your child is doing.

How you can help

- Place a large mat on the grass and let her lie and roll on it.
- If travelling in a pram, put sun block on your child at regular intervals.
- If the journey is short enough, walk rather than take the car.
- Take your child's toys outside and play there, rather than indoors, whenever the weather is suitable.

Think first! Never leave your child unattended in the garden or anywhere outside.

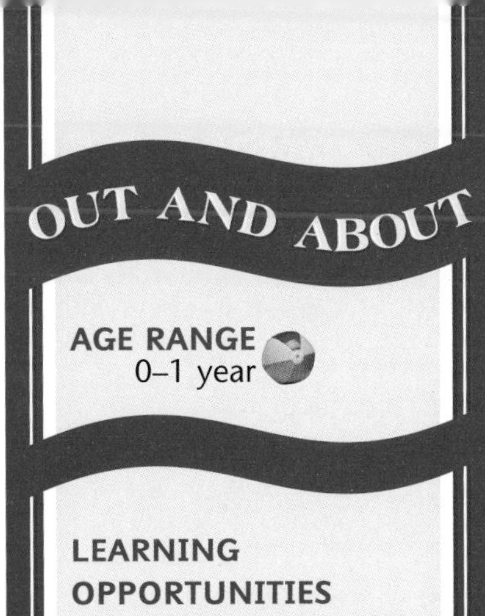

AGE RANGE
0–1 year

LEARNING OPPORTUNITIES
- To encourage stretching and reaching
- To provide visual stimulation
- To introduce patterns.

YOU WILL NEED
- Bells or pompoms; elastic; glue; paper plates or stiff card cut into discs or hexagons; felt-tipped pens.

Flying free

Sharing the game

- Draw bold patterns on to the discs or hexagons. Include spots, stripes, zigzags and so on.
- Make another set of disc or hexagons with basic faces on them, such as happy, sad, sleeping, winking and so on. Securely add bells or pompoms.
- Join the discs or hexagons on to lengths of elastic, tying them off carefully.
- Attach some of the shapes from the pram hood, above the car seat or on a bush near to your baby when he is in the garden.
- Help your baby to stretch and reach the bells or pompoms and watch them bounce away on the elastic.

- Hold a disc or hexagon and spin it around, take it near to your child, then let it go. Pretend to be surprised! Repeat with the various shapes.

Taking it further

- Laminate the shapes or use sticky-backed plastic to cover them. Let your baby hold them. Encourage him to watch you trace the patterns on them.
- Use some of the shapes and attachments to create a mobile. Hang it in areas where your baby can watch the items twirl and move in the wind.
- Use some old chimes or bells to add to the 'flyers'.

AGE RANGE
0–1 year

LEARNING OPPORTUNITIES
- To encourage visual tracking
- To introduce contrasts
- To develop curiosity.

YOU WILL NEED
Four plastic coat-hangers; coloured ribbons or lengths of fabric; small toys; everyday items; natural objects; elastic.

Hanging around

Sharing the game

- Cover a coat-hanger with a rainbow of coloured ribbons, leaving some lengths hanging. Hang a variety of bright, small toys from these. Place the coat-hanger somewhere your baby can watch it move gently.
- Cover the second coat-hanger with natural-toned ribbons and hang flowers, leaves and twigs from them. Place this near to the other coat-hanger. Twirl it or gently blow on it to make it move.

- Put white ribbons over the third coat-hanger and hang a toothbrush, comb and brush from them.
- Cover the fourth coat-hanger with silver ribbons. Hang some shiny objects from them.
- Hang these decorative 'mobiles' in places above where your baby sits in the garden, on her pram or from the washing line.
- Place one of the mobiles in a low position so that your baby can reach and explore the items. Ensure that all the items are very securely fastened. Alternate the mobiles so that they are in different positions on different occasions.

Taking it further

- Attach some of the various items to lengths of string or ribbon and tie them to a few wicker baskets. Let your baby explore them freely.
- Show your baby how the washing on the line blows dry on a windy day. Peg up some of her soft toys so that she can watch them sway in the breeze.

LEARNING OPPORTUNITIES

- To encourage control of body
- To encourage manipulation of materials
- To develop an appreciation of texture.

YOU WILL NEED

A large space (outdoor and grassy if possible); large wool rug; bright duvet cover; large length of lace or muslin fabric.

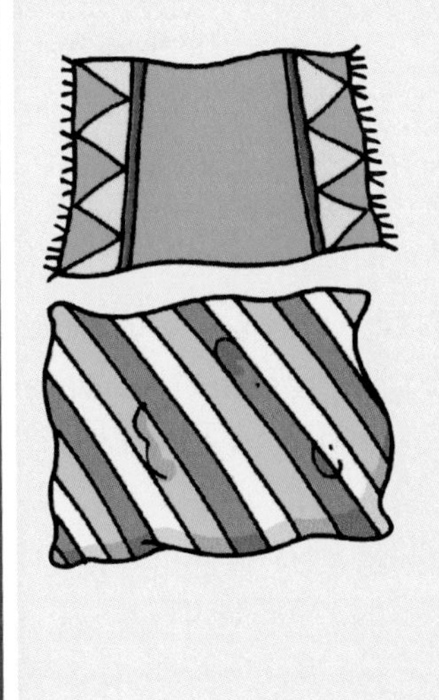

Move my body

Sharing the game

- Spread the various materials on the ground. Sit quietly with your baby on the grass or on one of the covers.
- While sitting on the grass, bounce your baby on your lap. Sing a little rhyme in time to the bouncing.
- Place him on the grass and rock him gently beside you, from side to side. Explain what you are doing as you carry out the movement.
- Count to three and then gently roll your baby over once. If he likes it, repeat a few times. Count before turning each time, as this will encourage him to anticipate the movement.
- Stand and help him to tiptoe through the grass. Repeat a few times in different directions. Explain what is happening. Take off both your own shoes and your baby's. Holding hands, walk together over each piece of material.
- Now sit on each piece. Encourage your baby to touch it and describe it to him as he does so.
- Lie your baby down and lie next to him. Roll away from him and then back again, making eye contact. Repeat this a few times if he enjoys it.
- Lie on your tummy and encourage him to do the same. Help him to turn over if necessary.

Taking it further

- For each part of the experience, stop and tickle your baby's toes, chin and so on.
- Stop every now and then and call his attention to what is next to you. Touch or lift things if appropriate.
- Raise your baby above the pieces of material and 'fly' him around.

OUT AND ABOUT

AGE RANGE
10–12 months

LEARNING OPPORTUNITIES
- To encourage self-help skills
- To introduce the idea of cause and effect
- To develop an interest in the natural world.

YOU WILL NEED
Sand tray; sand; soil; towels; water; basins or trays.

Clean up

Sharing the game

- If in a garden or outdoor-play space, select an appropriate area to place a pile of damp sand, a pile of damp soil and a basin of water. If indoors, place these materials into large trays, boxes or basins.
- Let your baby explore the sand and soil with her hands. After a short time, describe what she is feeling. Ask her questions about the feel of it. (Remember, you are not expecting an answer!)
- Take off both your own shoes and socks and your child's. Explain that you are going to stand in the sand. Encourage her to join you; if she does not want to, ask her to 'dip' her hands in and rub a little on her feet. Demonstrate what you mean so that she can copy. Let your child watch if she prefers to – never force her.
- Come out of the sand, take a towel and offer one to your baby, then try to wipe the wet sand off. Exclaim how difficult it is to remove the sand! Point to the water, but don't say anything. If she does not move towards the water, then suggest that you could wash your feet in it. Encourage her to copy you as you wet your feet in the basin of water.
- Repeat the whole experience with the soil. Offer the towel and see if your baby goes to the water to try to clean her feet.

Taking it further

- Instead of soil and sand, use 'gloop' (cornflour mixed with water, to which you can also add glitter), sawdust or paint.

OUT AND ABOUT

AGE RANGE
1–2 years

LEARNING OPPORTUNITIES
- To develop balance and control
- To develop hand–eye co-ordination
- To encourage manipulation of resources.

YOU WILL NEED
Chalk (or length of fabric or carpet, rope and A4-size snake face on paper or material); ball; beanbag.

Follow the snake

Sharing the game

- Use chalk to draw a snake shape on a paved or patio area. Alternatively, lay out some fabric or rope and attach the face shape.
- Ask your toddler to point to the face and then the tail.
- Invite him to walk along the snake, touch its face, then walk to its tail.
- Offer your toddler a ball and explain that he is going to stand at one end and you will stand at the other. Ask him which end he would like to stand at. Move to the opposite end and ask him to roll the ball to you. Repeat the game several times.
- Now walk to your toddler and ask him if he would like to swap the ball for a beanbag. If he does not want to, let him continue to roll the ball and introduce the beanbag when he is ready.
- Invite your toddler to try to roll the beanbag. When it doesn't work, ask him how he might be able to move it from one end of the snake to the other. Try his suggestion a few times. If he did not suggest throwing the beanbag, then suggest it to him now.

Taking it further

- Draw some food inside the snake's tummy, or stick down some visual aids along the length of the snake.
- Ask your toddler to stand on the tail and place objects nearby. Invite him to move (or jump) to the apple, the fish, the carrot and so on.
- Encourage your toddler to bounce the ball on or near to each item.

LEARNING OPPORTUNITIES
- To develop an appreciation of living things
- To encourage a sense of wonder
- To stimulate curiosity.

YOU WILL NEED
An area for walking and collecting natural objects; small bag, box or basket.

All around the world

Sharing the game

- Dress your toddler appropriately for a walk in the garden, park or wooded area.
- While out walking, call her attention to natural items, rubbish, wildlife and so on.
- Stand under a tree or near a bush and let her look at the leaves, blossoms and berries.
- Describe how they are moving. Ask her what it is that makes them move. Provide her with the answer if she doesn't know or cannot say.
- Gently pick up a leaf and some blossom from the ground. (Remember, it is illegal to pick wild flowers. Make sure that your child is aware of this from an early age.) Stress that you are not touching the berries because some of them are dangerous. Explain that the birds need some of them for food.
- Offer the leaf and blossom to your toddler and let her explore them. Invite her to place them into her bag when she is ready.
- Next, look for some pebbles. Encourage your toddler to choose one, or select one to inspect. Let her place it in her bag.
- Collect twigs and leaves, talking about their colours, textures and so on. Let your toddler place each item in her bag.

Taking it further

- On your return, ask your toddler to take one item out of her bag and to name it, describe it and place it on a table. Repeat with each item.
- Invite your toddler to select a large piece of paper and to glue each item on to it. Hang the collage in a place that she can readily return to – this will remind her of the walk that you did together.

AGE RANGE
1–2 years

LEARNING OPPORTUNITIES

- To become familiar with the natural world
- To develop vocabulary
- To develop appreciation of likes and dislikes.

YOU WILL NEED

Garden area; soil; flowers; grass; leaves; pebbles.

Walk here and there

Sharing the game

- Visit the garden and create a little natural 'obstacle course' with a pile of each of the item. Create a puddle of water if needed.
- Take your toddler on a walk to find the piles of items and let him explore them.
- Describe what the piles look like and feel like when touched. Encourage him to touch each item.
- Invite him to walk gently through the items. Repeat the walk, but this time more boisterously!
- Draw your toddler's attention to the sounds. Walk through a pile yourself and talk about the sounds that you have produced. Let your toddler walk through the next pile. Keep taking it in turns.
- Now suggest that you both take off your shoes and socks. Repeat the whole process, but this time paying attention to the way each pile feels, as well as to the sounds that it makes.
- Describe what you can feel under your feet. Encourage your toddler to join in by making facial expressions if he is can't describe with words.

Taking it further

- Give your toddler a little basket of flowers or pebbles and ask him to create a trail as he walks about the garden. After a short walk, stop and retrace your steps, encouraging him to find the path that he has created with the flowers or pebbles.

OUT AND ABOUT

AGE RANGE
1–2 years

LEARNING OPPORTUNITIES
- To encourage exploration
- To introduce the concept of length
- To develop an appreciation of space.

YOU WILL NEED
A basket; lengths of ribbon; garden area or room free of hazards.

Tie a yellow ribbon

Sharing the game

- Ask your toddler to place the basket on the floor, then invite her to explore the ribbons that you have put in it.
- Draw her attention to their colours, lengths and textures.
- Lay a few of the ribbons out on the floor and encourage your toddler to do the same. Introduce words such as 'long', 'longer', 'longest', 'short', 'shorter' and 'shortest'.
- Ask your toddler to select a ribbon that she likes, then place it on your shoulder. Choose one ribbon yourself and place it on her shoulder.
- Ask your toddler for some ideas for other places to hang the ribbons. Let her carry out her suggestions, or provide her with some suggestions for her to try out.
- Now invite your toddler to take the basket of ribbons outside. Sit on the grass together and ask her to choose her favourite ribbon. Can she choose one for you too?
- Explain that you are going to hang yours over the washing line. Ask her where she would like to hang hers.
- Now set some challenges for your toddler. Can she find the red/dark/longest ribbon? Encourage her to hang all the ribbons around the garden – on tree branches, around a trunk, over a bush, around a planter, over a garden chair, from a door handle and so on.

Taking it further

- Fill a plant pot with soil. Place a small branch from a bush or tree (from your garden) into it. Provide your toddler with lengths of ribbon, wool and string and encourage her to use them to decorate the branch.

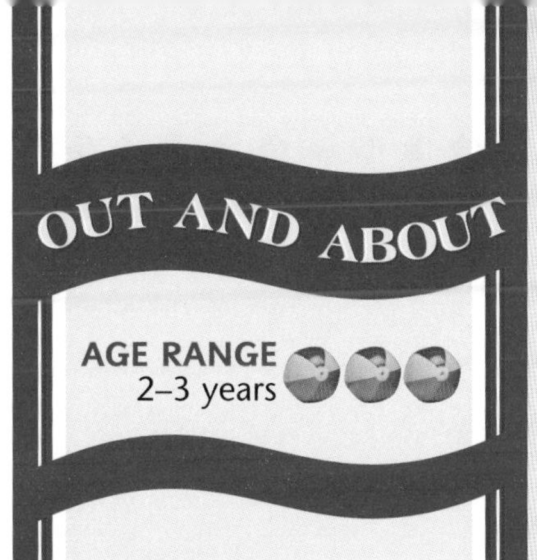

AGE RANGE
2–3 years

LEARNING OPPORTUNITIES

- To encourage understanding of weather
- To encourage communication
- To relate to the world around him.

YOU WILL NEED

A pin board; large piece of brightly-coloured card or magnetic boar; bag containing small (A5 size) visual aids showing weather types, such as a sun, a grey cloud with rain drops, a white cloud with snowdrops and a tree bending over (it is a good idea to laminate these, or to cover them with sticky-backed plastic).

What weather?

Sharing the game

- Sit with your child and talk about the type of weather it is outside. Go to the window or door and look at the sky, the bushes and the trees. Are there any puddles? Look for signs of the weather together.
- Sit down again and take out your bag of visual aids. Offer the bag to your child and ask him to select one of the pictures. Invite him to describe what he has chosen. Ask him whether it matches the weather today.
- Repeat the process with each picture. Ask your child what he thinks about this kind of weather each time. Does he like to play outside when it is like that?
- Now show your child the pin board and suggest that you choose the correct picture(s) to tell today's weather story. Go back to the door or window to look out again and challenge him to pick the correct picture.

Taking it further

- Sing a song about the weather while holding the visual aids.
- Fill a bag with items relating to the weather, such as sun-glasses, wellington boots, a scarf, hat and umbrella. If possible, include some pictures from books or magazines of children wearing these items. Talk about the items and match them to the pictures.

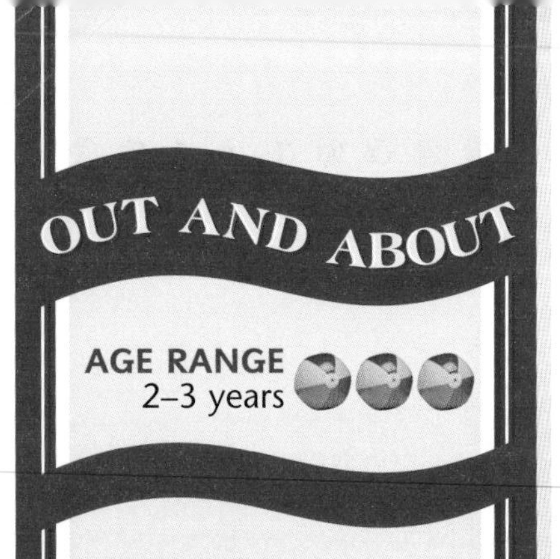

AGE RANGE
2–3 years

LEARNING OPPORTUNITIES

- To encourage an awareness of differences
- To introduce the concept of living and non-living
- To develop an appreciation of the natural world.

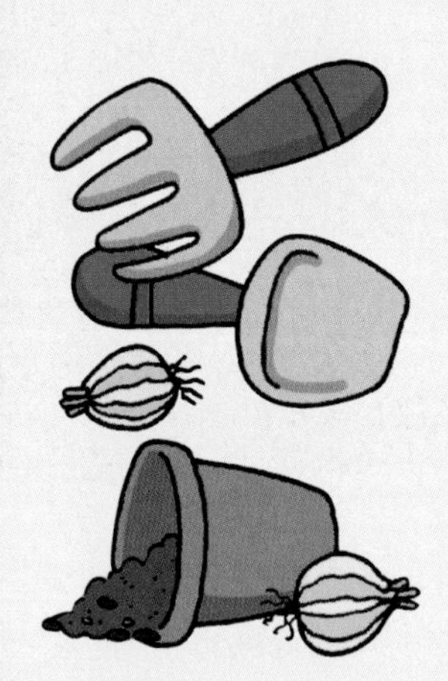

YOU WILL NEED

Two large trays; bags of soil; plastic flower pots in different sizes; plastic flowers; children's plastic garden tools; fork; spoon; wooden spoon; ladle; flower bulbs and the pictures of the flowers that they will grow into; small watering can.

Soil play

Sharing the game

- Place the two large trays on the ground outside and place the bags of soil near them.
- Show your child the various 'tools' and invite her to choose one to move the soil into the trays. Do this together and when each tray is half-full, ask her if that is enough. If she wants to add more, let her continue for a short time before suggesting that she stop and try something else.
- Offer your child the water to pour into one of the trays. Stress that you want her to add water to only one of them. Help her to pour it if necessary.
- Let her explore the differences between the two trays, then show her the various pots. Invite her to play with these. Fill a few with soil and let her copy if she wants to.
- After one or two of the pots have some soil in, offer your child the plastic flowers to 'plant'.
- Now offer her the bulbs, showing her the pictures of the flowers that they will grow into. Let her plant the bulbs and water them.

Taking it further

- Gather a range of flowers from your garden, or buy a few bunches (preferably ones with strong stalks). Put a bit of oasis into the bottom of a pot and allow your child to create an arrangement for the table.

AGE RANGE
2–3 years

LEARNING OPPORTUNITIES
- To encourage sorting and matching
- To promote an awareness of foods
- To encourage mark-making.

YOU WILL NEED
Labels from cans of food; empty wrappers and packets; notebook; glue; pencil.

Shopping list

Sharing the game

- Over the course of a week, keep empty food packets or labels from tins (preferably some of your child's favourites).
- Spread the labels and wrappers out on a table-top and sit down at the table with your child.
- Ask him to select something that he would like to buy at the shop and encourage him to glue the picture into his notebook. Repeat this several times.
- Make some more suggestions to your child and ask him to 'note them down' in the notebook with the pencil. Encourage him to make some marks on the page.
- Now go to a shop with your child. When in the shop, ask him if he would like to remind you of what you need by showing you the pages in his notebook, or by telling you what you decided together.
- Let him go along the aisles with you, prompting him if necessary. Encourage him to mark off each item as you put it into your basket or trolley (be prepared for this to take some time!).

Taking it further

- Buy two of each item and on returning home, take the labels from one set of items as you use them. Cut out the main parts of the labels and stick each one on to a separate piece of card. Create a shop with the matching unused items. Offer your child the list and a bag and invite him to 'go shopping'.

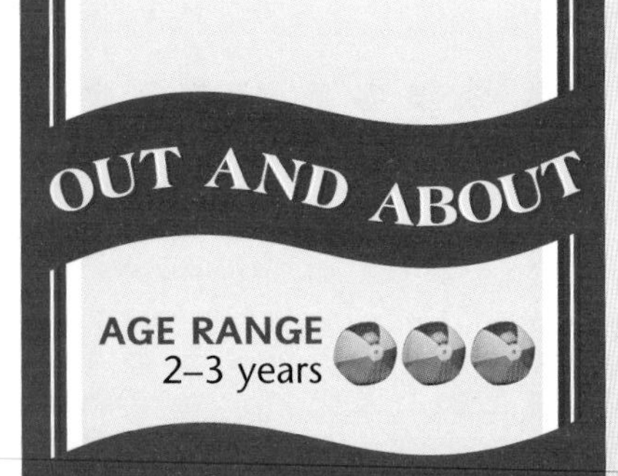

AGE RANGE
2–3 years

LEARNING OPPORTUNITIES
- To develop the senses
- To explore the natural world
- To develop vocabulary.

YOU WILL NEED
An outdoor area, preferably with grass, bushes, trees and flowers; masking tape.

Nature bracelet

Sharing the game

- Go outside with your child and walk around drawing her attention to the various natural grasses and plants.
- Invite her to touch some and smell them if appropriate (be aware which plants are poisonous).
- Ask your child if she would like to make a little bracelet from some of the things that she has just looked at.
- Create a bracelet each by wrapping masking tape loosely around her wrist and around yours, making sure that the sticky side of the tape is not against the skin.
- If your child is not happy with the tape being put around her wrist, ask her to help you to place it around the outside of a plastic cup.
- Next, go around the area again, this time encouraging your child to gently pick just a little piece of grass, a herb leaf or a flower. Stress that if we pick too many, the garden will not look nice any more – explain to her that you are just picking enough for the bracelet or to decorate the cup ring.
- When your child is happy that she has gathered enough items, sit together on the grass and attach the natural items to the masking tape. Invite her to name each of the items that she has gathered. Admire each other's bracelets and encourage her to share her opinions on which she likes the most, which ones smell nice, what colour is the brightest and so on.

Taking it further

- Gather the items in plastic cups, then invite your child to glue them on to a piece of paper or card to create a small garden of her own.

CHAPTER 5

LET'S PRETEND

Using stories and poems will help your child to understand the world, his place in it and the events that happen in his daily life. In addition, by acting out stories through role-play, your child will be trying out new ideas and practising new words and behaviours in a pretend situation before using them in the 'real' world. Role-play can help to give your child confidence and a sense of identity, and will help him to understand how he fits into the world.
The games in this chapter will help you to provide role-play situations and gives you plenty of ideas for sharing stories and rhymes with your child.

THE POSSIBILITIES OF STORY

From the moment he is is born, your baby learns about his world. As he grows older he will explore it in more depth and in many different ways. All this time he will be developing skills and concepts. At the same time, and from a very early age, you can introduce your child to the wider world – through stories, songs and poems. As you read and share these stories and rhymes, you will be encouraging his awareness of other people, the jobs that they do, the way that they speak and the way that they look. Your child will be learning about his world in a safe and secure environment – through role-play, rather than by first-hand experience. As a result of listening to stories and rhymes, and through taking part in role-play, your child will be interacting with you and the characters that he comes across. He will gather ideas, develop a picture of his world and begin to use his imagination.

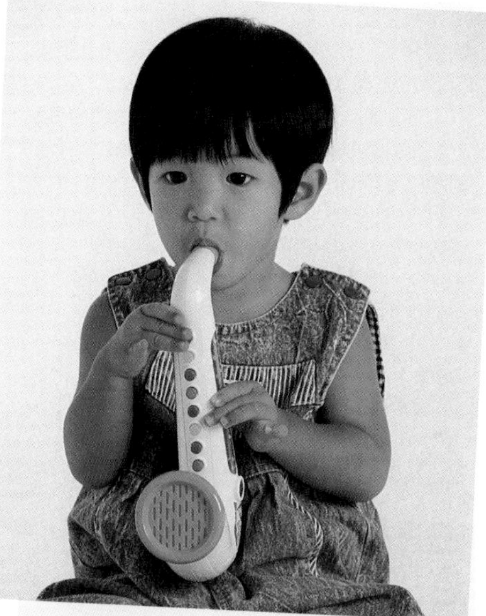

By encouraging your young child to respond to books, pictures and words, you are introducing him to the delights of reading. Babies from a very early age will enjoy sharing books, eagerly pointing to pictures and naming what they see. They will love the close comfort of hearing your voice and will delight in hearing you bring the stories enthusiastically to life, with sound effects and actions.

Using books as a stimulus for role-play is a relaxed and informal approach to reading. Your young child will have a natural interest in responding to stories, songs and poems, especially if they are presented in an interesting manner.

How you can help

- Sing songs every day with your young child. Add actions, sound effects and visual aids to relate to the songs and bring them to life.
- Use rhymes to introduce new vocabulary and new people to your young child.
- Use simple story-books as a visual stimulus to develop pretend-play situations. For example, a story about a bus could lead to some imaginative play where you might be the bus driver and your child could sit behind you. Together you could make the sound of the engine and arrange for money to be paid for a ticket.
- Tell stories that involve your young child. It may relate to something that he has seen happen. You could transport him into the situation by making up a story.

BECOMING SOMEONE ELSE

If you encourage your child to become involved in pretend play – to respond to others and imitate others – he may learn how to 'become' somebody or something else, or believe that he is somewhere else. When he talks and communicates through a pretend telephone, he is using the language acquired from listening to others around him. He has learned how to imitate the roles of other people he knows. This ability shows that he is beginning to make sense of the world around him.

Puppets can also be used to encourage imaginative play and stimulate your child's imagination. Put a variety of finger puppets, home-made puppets and glove puppets in a box to use with your child. Make some simple puppets yourself using everyday materials, by drawing faces on to wooden spoons or paper bags, or by simply cutting out magazine pictures and sticking them on to straws or sticks.

By taking part in pretend play with your young child, you will be helping him to develop his imagination through fantasy worlds. He will start to learn the difference between real and pretend worlds, and he will find this fun!

Set up situations when you invite your child to 'pretend' that he is helping to set the table, eat lunch, wash the dishes, dress a baby and so on. Do these activities alongside your child and make sure that you use language and gestures to encourage him to carry out tasks.

How you can help

- Gather pictures of farm, wild and pet animals so that you can encourage your child to 'become' these animals.
- Having been out and seen a fire engine, car or crossing-patrol attendant, encourage your child to 'pretend' that he is these objects or people.
- Use aids such as a till, tool kit and chalk and chalkboard to stimulate your child into taking on a role.
- Play role-play games together – for example, ask him to pretend that he is brushing his teeth or combing his hair.
- Act out some everyday chores such as dusting or driving the car, and ask your child to guess what you are doing.
- Invite your child to join you as you pretend to get washed or dressed, or to eat lunch. Your child will quickly become more confident if you do these activities together.

DRESSING UP

Most young children love the thrill of dressing up and pretending to be somebody else. The delight of trying on daddy's shoes, mummy's scarf or granny's glasses is clear to see as your child takes on any of these pretend roles. Encourage him to get involved with this kind of fantasy play by joining in with him. This will help him to gain confidence and to become more involved in the role-play games.

This type of experience, as well as being fun, will help your child in a number of ways. As a direct result of fantasy play, he will usually find it easier to share materials and work with others, use a variety of language, try out new ideas and use objects to represent other things.

How you can help

- Provide a box of old clothes for your child to use for dressing-up games. Include some old hats, coats and outdoor things.
- Dress up with your child and show him how you use your voice to pretend to be someone else.
- Make or buy some masks to wear. Show your child how to put them on and pretend to be someone else.
- Provide a paper dolly and paper clothes for some cut-out dressing-up fun. Dress a doll in different outfits and pretend that she is doing different jobs.
- Use small-world toys to pretend exciting adventures.

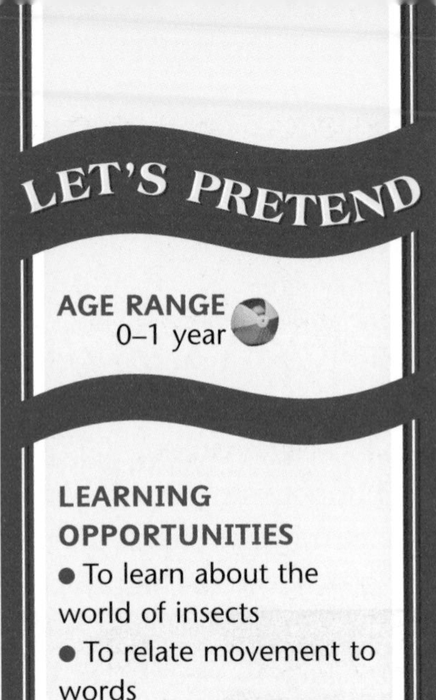

LET'S PRETEND

AGE RANGE
0–1 year

LEARNING OPPORTUNITIES

- To learn about the world of insects
- To relate movement to words
- To develop ability to listen and concentrate.

YOU WILL NEED

A comfortable place in which to sit opposite your baby; A4-sized photographs or pictures of an ant, butterfly, ladybird and worm (hand puppets of these minibeasts would be even more fun!).

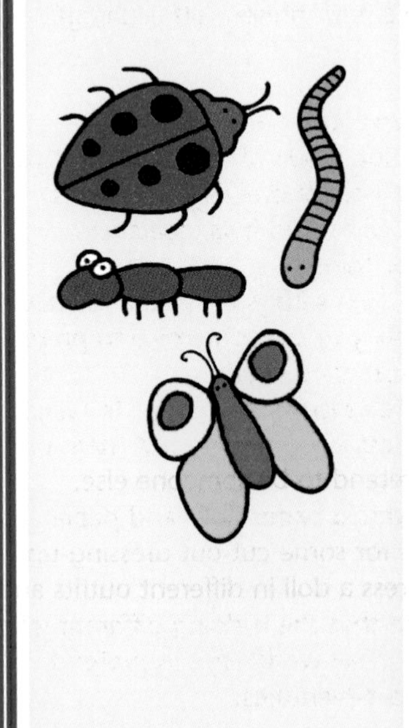

In my palm

Sharing the game

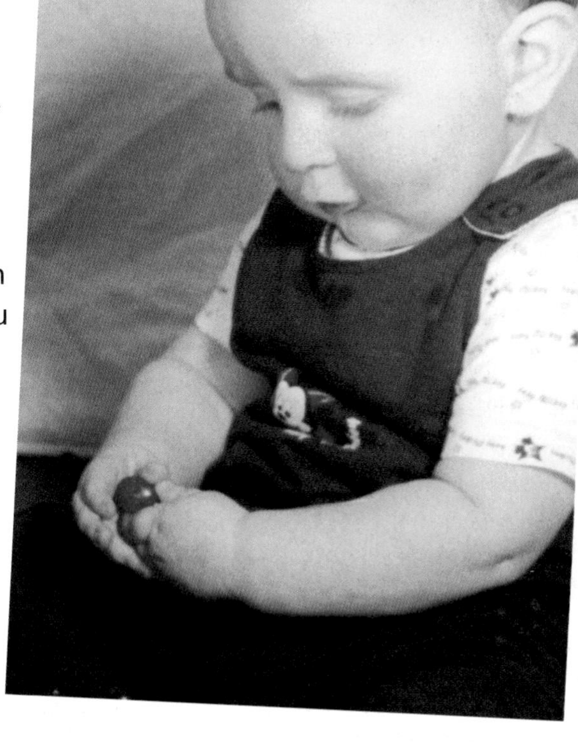

- Look at the photos or puppets with your baby.
- Talk about the minibeasts' colours and sizes, and about the way that they move.
- Hold out your hand, place one of the photos or puppets on your palm and say, 'In my hand you can find little animals of every kind'.
- Gently place the photo or puppet beside your baby so that he can still see it.
- Hold your baby's hand gently in yours and repeat the refrain. While saying the words, gently stroke his palm against yours. Say the refrain again, adding at the end, 'An ant goes marching'. Change your stroking to a 'marching' movement!
- Repeat the verse, each time adding a line and some more movements, for example, 'A butterfly flutters' (gently tickle your baby's cheeks and chin); 'A ladybird skips' (tickle along his arms and legs) and 'A worm wriggles' (tickle his head and tummy).
- When you have introduced each minibeast, let your baby explore the photos or puppets. Each time he chooses a new picture, name it for him.

Taking it further

- Use a different set of animal pictures or puppets and change movements to suit the animals, adding sounds as appropriate.
- Walk around the garden or a park with your baby. See if you can spot some real minibeasts. Draw his attention to them.

AGE RANGE
0–1 year

LEARNING OPPORTUNITIES
- To introduce routines in a fun way
- To develop vocabulary
- To stimulate a sense of curiosity.

YOU WILL NEED
A hand puppet or one of your baby's favourite soft toys; items for changing your baby.

Puppet time

Sharing the game

- When you are getting ready to change your baby, sit on the floor next to her, along with the puppet or teddy.
- Explain that you are going to change her.
- Pretend to talk to the puppet, asking the puppet to help you gather the items that you need. Each time the puppet moves to fetch an item, tell your baby what the puppet is doing. Say where the puppet is going and what the item is called. Thank the puppet for all its help.
- Once you have placed all the required items near to your baby, put the puppet down. Explain that the puppet is tired now. Then tell your baby that it is time to change her.
- Explain each part of the changing routine as you carry it out. Do not expect your baby to understand, but she will enjoy listening to your soothing tone.

Taking it further

- Use the puppet to help you again when your baby is sitting in her high chair. Make the puppet help you to set the table, stir the food and spoon the food out. Make it pretend to eat some.
- Offer your baby her own spoon to encourage her to 'copy' the puppet. Explain and describe exactly what the puppet is doing.

AGE RANGE
0–1 year

LEARNING OPPORTUNITIES
- To encourage use of imagination
- To develop hand–eye co-ordination
- To relate items to purpose.

YOU WILL NEED
A box; sponge nose; pretend glasses; sun-glasses; fancy hat; pretend beard; sparkly beads; crown; mirror.

Put it on

Sharing the game

- Sit your baby on the floor and place the box of goodies beside him. Let him explore the items in the box. Each time he selects an item, name it.

- Choose one of the items and put it on. Name the item and describe it – what it feels like, its colour, where you have placed it and what it is for.
- Repeat with a few of the other items. Offer each one to your baby and encourage him to try to put it on. Help him if necessary.
- Now put on each item, one at a time, and say, 'Hello little Joe (use your baby's name). Do you like my sparkly beads?' or 'Do you like my fancy hat?'. Try using a different tone and accent as you change the resources.
- Put one of the items on your baby, then hold him up to a mirror to show him what he looks like. Repeat with another item if he enjoys the game.

Taking it further

- Choose one of your baby's favourite board books. Try to bring it to life by finding real-life items that go with the story, such as a toy duck or dog, a flower or a toy boat.

AGE RANGE
0–1 year

LEARNING OPPORTUNITIES
- To introduce story and visual aids
- To develop listening and concentration skills
- To bring stories to life.

YOU WILL NEED
A brightly-coloured book such as *Come on Daisy!* by Jane Simmons (Orchard Books); props to go with the story, such as a soft toy duck, a toy fish, a toy mouse and a toy frog; brightly-coloured pillowcase.

Bring it to life

Sharing the game

- Sit with your baby on your knee or opposite you on the floor.
- Show her the cover of the book that you have chosen. Describe what is on it (for example, the colours, the water, the duck and the plants).
- As you turn the pages of the book, make suitable sounds and actions for Daisy. Make quacking sounds and flap your hands on your baby's knee, pretending that they are Daisy's feet flapping! Stand up and say that you are walking like Daisy, waddling about in front of your baby.
- Turn the page to the little mouse. Squeak, then 'scamper' your hands over the page, over your baby's legs, and tickle your baby under the chin.
- Look at the page with the fish. Move your hand in an undulating fashion to simulate a fish swimming. Open and close your mouth to pretend that you are a fish!
- Now read the page where the frog appears. Make hopping movements with your hands. Move your hands over the page and over your baby's legs. Use the toys and your voice to give the story as much life as possible.
- Use this technique with a variety of books. Bring the characters to life with props, noises and actions. Soon your baby will be joining in with you!

Taking it further

- Choose a few of your baby's favourite books and create a bag of objects to go with each book.

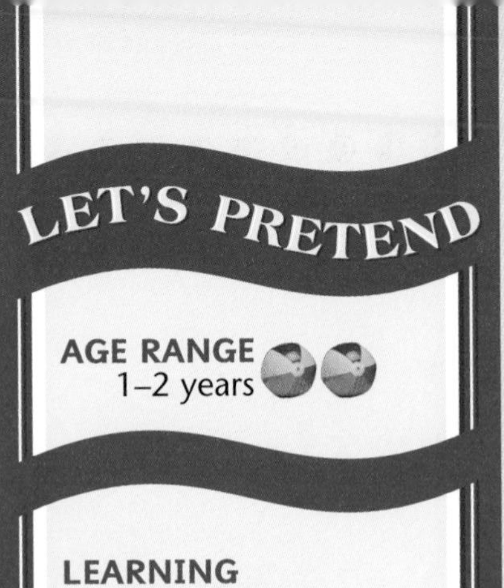

AGE RANGE
1–2 years

LEARNING OPPORTUNITIES
- To stimulate the sense of sight
- To develop natural curiosity
- To encourage exploration.

YOU WILL NEED
Four or five boxes in different shapes and sizes; variety of large buttons and buckles; fancy shoe; sequinned cummerbund; jewelled tiara; large shells; selection of bright ribbons.

THINK FIRST!
Make sure that there is nothing small or sharp that your child may choke on or hurt himself with.

Wonder boxes

Sharing the game

- Put the items into some boxes.
- Set out the boxes so that your toddler can explore the contents. Put lids on some of the boxes and leave some slightly open.
- Sit with your toddler and present each box to him. Slightly open the lid of the first box so that he can just see what is inside.
- Leave the next box closed so that he can discover for himself what is inside.
- Encourage your toddler to explore the contents of the boxes. Spread out the objects and play with them together. Describe them to your toddler.

- Turn some of the boxes upside-down and hide the contents for your toddler to find.
- Put all the contents into one box so that it overflows. Take out a few of the items and offer them to your toddler.
- Gently tap a box and encourage your toddler to put an item inside. Then ask him to sort out the items into different boxes.

Taking it further

- Put a range of your toddler's clothes in a box.
- Put his cutlery, bowl and cup in another box. Fill yet another box with some of his bath toys.

LET'S PRETEND

AGE RANGE
1–2 years

LEARNING OPPORTUNITIES
- To develop vocabulary
- To introduce the idea of a game
- To introduce groupings of objects.

YOU WILL NEED
A large tray; cup; spoon; bowl; teddy; banana; bread; yoghurt; bright piece of fabric.

What's hiding?

Sharing the game

- Place the tray on the floor beside your toddler. Put the cup, the spoon and the bowl on to the tray. Name each item as you put it down.
- Cover the items with the fabric.
- Gently and slowly uncover each item, encouraging your toddler to name it. Alternatively, name it yourself and encourage her to repeat the word after you.
- Invite your toddler to show you the spoon, give you the bowl and pick up the cup.
- Let your toddler explore the items and encourage her to feed Teddy with them.
- Repeat the process, this time using the banana, the bread and the yoghurt.
- Let your toddler watch as you cut the banana and bread up, and spoon some yoghurt into the bowl.
- Cover the foods, then gently uncover one piece of food at a time. Name each food and encourage your toddler to pretend to feed Teddy.
- Invite her to eat some herself, putting out a fresh selection for her to choose from.

Taking it further

- Choose four of your toddler's favourite play things. Place them on the tray and cover them with the material. Uncover and talk about each item in turn.
- Repeat with a shoe, sock, slipper and boot. Each time, encourage your toddler to name the item.

LEARNING OPPORTUNITIES

- To encourage pretend play
- To develop the idea that people have different roles
- To encourage listening and responding.

YOU WILL NEED

A woolly hat; policeman's hat; crown; clown's hat; selection of scarves; mirror; large bag.

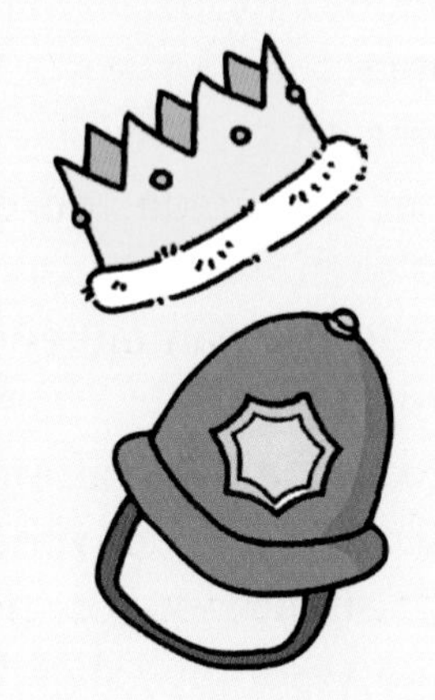

Hats off

Sharing the game

- Place all the hats and scarves in the large bag.
- Sit on the floor with your toddler. Create enough space to spread out the contents of the bag on the floor.
- Choose a hat from the bag and offer it to your toddler. Describe the hat and talk about who would be likely to wear it.
- Select another hat and put it on. Play the role of the owner, saying, for example, 'Hello, I'm a police officer, how can I help you?'.
- Continue to choose hats and put them on. Describe each hat to your toddler and take on the role of the person who would wear it, saying something relevant.
- Now choose a scarf and say something about it, such as, 'Oh my, it is cold today' or 'Do you like my beautiful scarf?'.
- Use your voice to create different people while wearing the different scarves.

Taking it further

- Find some books that show characters wearing clothes such as scarves and hats. Provide your toddler with a similar hat or scarf and encourage him to pretend to be one of the characters from the book as you look at it together.

LET'S PRETEND

AGE RANGE
1–2 years

LEARNING OPPORTUNITIES

- To introduce a sense of animal groups
- To encourage an awareness of shape and shadow
- To identify animals from clues.

YOU WILL NEED

Clear illustrations of animals (a set each of domestic, wild and farm animals); tracing paper; plain paper; black ink pen; card; glue; scissors.

Shadow cards

Sharing the game

- Choose four pet animals such as a cat, dog, rabbit and bird. Trace the basic outlines of the animals, using basic picture books for inspiration, or colouring books to trace over.
- Colour in the animal outlines with a black pen to create silhouettes. Glue the pictures on to card.
- Now show your toddler one of the animal 'shadows'.
- Make the sound of the animal for your toddler and ask her to guess what animal it is. Let her see the original illustrations of the animals and ask her to try to find the matching one.
- Repeat for the other animals. As your toddler matches the silhouette and picture of each animal, say the animal's name and make its sound. Encourage your toddler to join in with you.

- Create a set of wild animals. An elephant, a giraffe, a tiger and a crocodile would be ideal. Once more, create a set of silhouettes for these wild animals.
- Repeat the matching game. Encourage your toddler to make the animal sounds and name the animals.
- Finally, repeat the process, this time with a farm-animal set, for example, a cow, sheep, horse and pig.

Taking it further

- Mix up the three sets, including some of the original pictures as well as the silhouettes. Help your toddler to put two from each set together and encourage her to give the name or make the animal sound for each animal as well.

AGE RANGE
2–3 years

LEARNING OPPORTUNITIES

- To encourage participation
- To encourage role-play
- To develop a sense of fun.

YOU WILL NEED

A box; animal print paper or fabric; wild-animal cards or small soft toys; copy of the following poem:

Here is a box, let's open the lid.
I wonder whatever inside is hid.
Oh, it's a..., without a doubt.
Let's open the lid and let it out!

Here is a box

Sharing the game

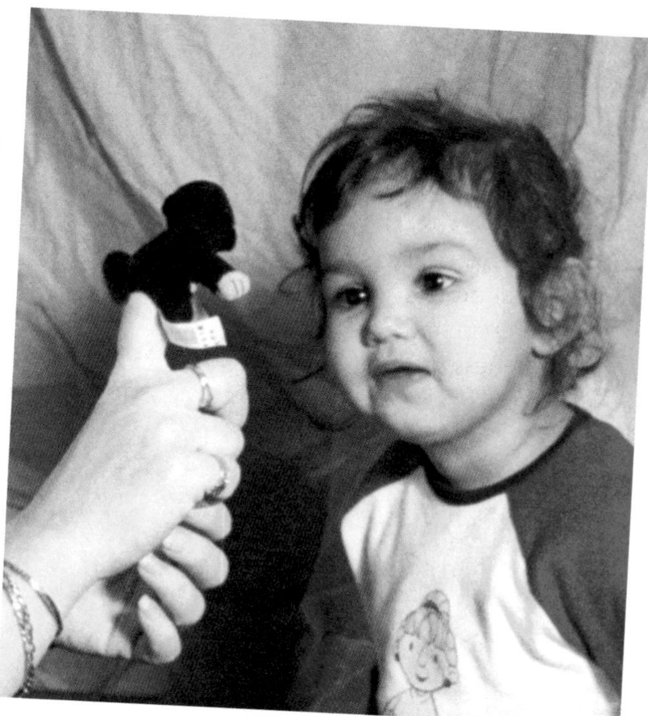

- Sit with your child on the floor.
- Put down the box of animal cards or toys for him to explore. Let him take them out and play with them.
- After a few minutes, ask your child to help you to put the animals back into the box. If he is not keen to do this, just replace some of them, allowing him to play with the remaining ones.
- Lift the box right up, beside your cheek, and start to say the rhyme to your child, adding the following actions:

  Here is a box (*tap the top*), let's open the lid. (*lift the lid and peep inside, closing it quickly*)
  I wonder whatever inside is hid.
  Oh it's a... (*take out one of the animals and invite your child to name it*), without a doubt.
  Let's open the lid and let it out! (*invite your child to take the animal out of the box*)

- Once your child has named the animal, encourage him to make its sound. Show him how to move around the room, the way that the animal would.

Taking it further

- Create another set of boxes with different sets of characters, such as people who help us or characters from favourite cartoons or traditional nursery rhymes.

AGE RANGE
2–3 years

LEARNING OPPORTUNITIES
- To develop gross motor skills
- To develop hand–eye co-ordination
- To listen and respond to instructions.

YOU WILL NEED
Large coloured hoops, or cardboard to create large hoops; string or ribbon; balls; beanbags; washing line or rope.

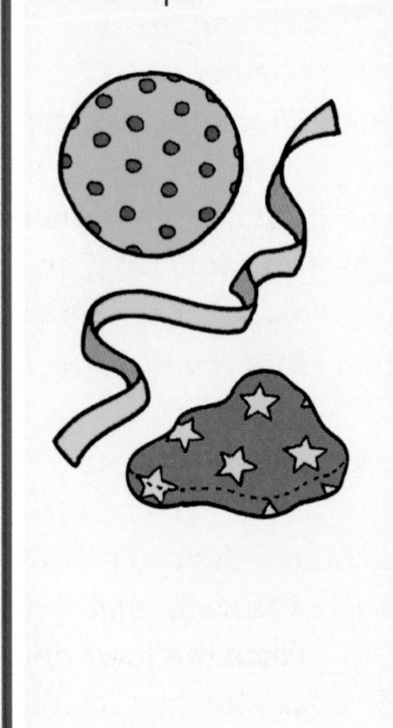

Circus hoops

Sharing the game

- Place the large hoops on the grass.
- Encourage your child to step from one hoop to the next. Ask her to stand in the green one, move to the red, then jump in the blue. (If you do not have coloured hoops, tie coloured ribbons to the hoops and explain that you will refer to the hoop with the green ribbon as the green hoop and so on.)
- Sit in one of the hoops and invite your child to sit in another.
- Show your child how to raise the hoop over her head. Ask her to copy you. Repeat the game a few times, before placing the hoop back on the ground. Now crawl to another hoop and ask your child to do the same.
- Stand in this hoop and raise it up over your body and over your head, then over your child's head. Now ask your child to move the hoop up her body, over her head and then back over your head. You will have to bend to allow her to do this!
- Next, use some string or ribbon to attach the hoops securely to a washing line or rope. Make sure that the hoop is hung above your child's head, so that she does not catch herself in it. Pass or throw balls and beanbags through the hoop.

Taking it further

- Place the large hoops back on the grass or lean them slightly against a box or small wall. Use the balls and beanbags to throw into the hoops. Move a little further away from them each time.

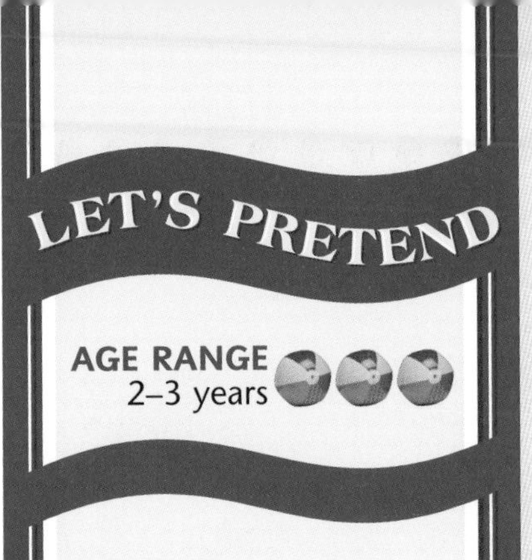

AGE RANGE
2–3 years

LEARNING OPPORTUNITIES

- To encourage matching skills
- To encourage sorting and categorising skills
- To develop vocabulary.

YOU WILL NEED

A low table; toy cash register; two shopping bags; range of toiletries, fruit and groceries (at least two of each kind).

Sort the shopping

Sharing the game

- Place a range of items on the table beside the cash register.
- Invite your child to 'go shopping'. Suggest that you each have a bag to carry your groceries and other items. (You may use plastic or toy food, but using the real thing is usually more exciting!)
- Tell your child that you need an apple. Ask him to pass you one and to place it in your bag for you. Now invite him to choose an item himself and challenge him to name it. Can he tell you what it is for?
- Repeat this a few times, offering praise and encouragement even when he gets the selection wrong.

- Now change the game slightly. Explain to your child that this time you would like him to put everything back in the 'shop'. Ask him to put all the matching items together.
- Sort the shopping further by asking him to put all the fruit or tins together. Can he put all of the things that you can't eat together?

Taking it further

- Take turns to be the shopkeeper. Place the food on one table and sit or stand beside the 'counter table'. Invite your child to name or describe what he would like, before passing the item to him to put in his shopping bag.
- Go on a visit to a shop and ask your child to hand you certain items and to select a few that he would like.

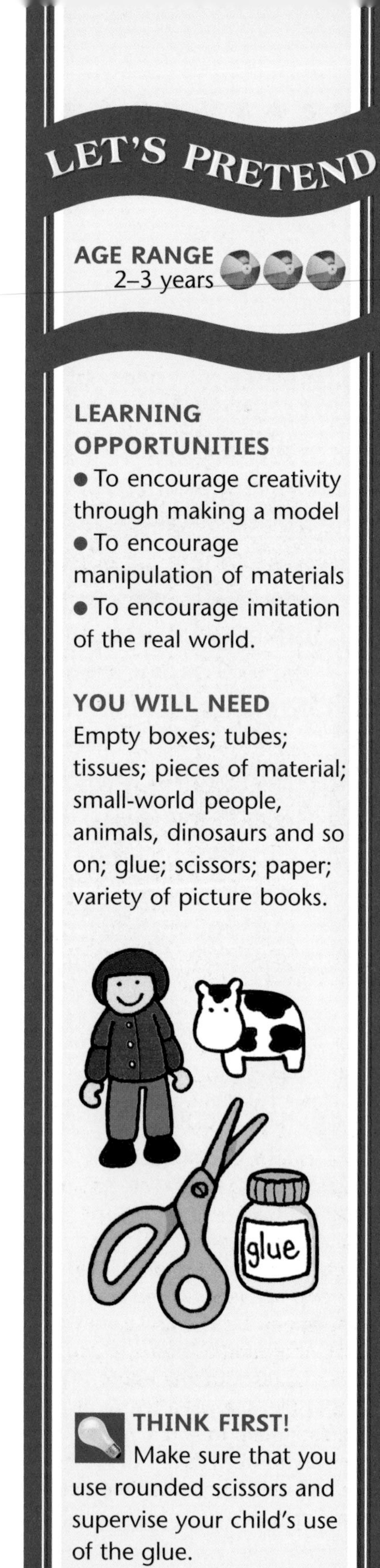

LET'S PRETEND

AGE RANGE
2–3 years

LEARNING OPPORTUNITIES
- To encourage creativity through making a model
- To encourage manipulation of materials
- To encourage imitation of the real world.

YOU WILL NEED
Empty boxes; tubes; tissues; pieces of material; small-world people, animals, dinosaurs and so on; glue; scissors; paper; variety of picture books.

THINK FIRST!
Make sure that you use rounded scissors and supervise your child's use of the glue.

Small world

Sharing the game

- Invite your child to select a range of small-world people and animals. Limit the number to two or three of each kind.
- Place all the materials on a low table and explain to your child that you would like to use them to make something for the animals. Ask her if she has any suggestions.
- Look at a few books with pictures of houses, boats, trees and so on to give your child some ideas. If she is struggling to suggest anything, help her by placing one of the small-world toys inside a small box. Suggest that this would make, for example, a nice kennel for a toy dog. But explain that it needs to be made cosy. Help her to join in with suggestions for making it more comfortable.
- Now encourage your child to think of an idea of her own, prompting her if necessary. Let her select some materials and invite her to use the scissors to cut things and the glue to stick things together. Help her whenever required.
- Once your child has made a start on her model, stay close by to help her to fix things together and to achieve the look that she is after!

Taking it further

- Encourage your child to use paint, pens and crayons to colour the model when it is finished.
- Use plastic containers to add to the model, creating a lake or river where water can be added.

CHAPTER 6

Even the youngest child enjoys investigating and exploring the world around her. As a parent or carer, wherever possible, you should strive to present your child with opportunities to make her own discoveries about her world every day.
In this chapter you will find a store of games and activities that encourage your child to explore her world, be it through her toys or through objects that she is in contact with every day.

LET'S GET BUSY

COMMONPLACE OBJECTS

Even the most everyday and trivial items are new to a young child. Babies and toddlers can be actively encouraged to use their senses to develop an awareness of the size, shape, texture and colour of objects. These objects do not need to be the very latest colourful and expensive toys, but may simply be more commonplace, such as a wooden spoon, some photographs or an empty feeding bottle.

Think first! If an item is not intended specifically for a baby or young child, make sure that it poses no risk to your child, particularly in terms of its potential as a choking hazard.

From around her third month, a baby begins to watch objects more carefully, stretching out towards anything that she sees. By the fifth month, she may firmly grasp a small toy in her hand, beginning to explore its form using touch and perhaps by trying to chew it. As she approaches her first birthday, she will use her hands to explore her toys and surroundings, developing her pincer grip between thumb and forefinger, and small muscles for fine control. At around this time, if you offer her boxes with interesting objects inside, she will attempt to manipulate them to find a way in. She will try to pull lids off, shake the boxes and put things into them once they are opened.

How you can help

- Take a selection of pots, plastic cups, wooden spoons, curtain rings and napkin rings, and place them in a box for your child to explore.
- Cut holes in lids of crisp tubes, taping any ragged edges, and offer your child plastic spoons or similar items for her to drop into the tube.
- Provide your child with some empty tubs and plastic plates, and give her a large box of everyday items for her to sort and choose from.

The mental and physical development of your child is rapid at this age. She will be gaining increasing control over her grasp and, as well as 'making her mark', it is likely that she will also be able to put small objects into jars and bottles, use a spoon to feed herself, thread large beads, and attempt simple inset puzzles.

MARK-MAKING

Between the ages of one and two, your child might also begin to use pencils, crayons and paint to make marks (sometimes on paper!). She will take great delight in her 'scribbles' and in watching, as you take your pencil 'for a walk' around a clean piece of paper.

Drawing is an excellent and important method of self-expression for a child. The more opportunity she is given to draw, the better her control of making marks will be. With this ability to make marks, your child will be able to realise her visual imagination on paper.

How you can help

- Offer your child pencils, crayons, charcoal, pastels and paints for her to make marks.
- Take a tray or table-top and spread out some paint, sand, lightly-whipped cream or custard with your hand. Encourage your child to make marks in it.
- Provide different types of paper such as sugar paper, silver foil, rice paper, and blotting paper, and encourage your child to 'write' on them.
- Offer your child paint, paper, a toothbrush, hairbrush, nail brush and shoe brush. Allow her to experiment with them.

THINK ABOUT IT

At around eighteen months, your child will attempt to partially dress herself and she will try more complex object manipulation. By the age of two, her pincer grip will be considerably more refined and she will be more confident in completing tasks demanding this skill. Eventually, towards her third birthday, she will attempt to cut with scissors, draw simple shapes and do up her own buttons.

While you are with your child, it is best to focus on what she can already do with confidence. Once you feel that she is happy with an activity, move on to something a little more challenging. Repeating a game or activity and consolidating the experience is often the best way to build a child's confidence while helping her to learn. Although she may appear to have mastered something today, it is quite normal and common that she may not seem as confident tomorrow. The more a skill is used, the more it develops – practice really does make perfect!

How you can help

- Offer your child items that she has to push, pull, screw, tap, prod or dial to make something happen.
- Take small items and play 'Magic'. Hide the item in one hand, challenging your child to guess in which one it is. Next, hide it under your leg or a beaker and invite her to find the hiding place.
- Sit with your child and draw a large simple picture of a house, fish or face. Cut it into two pieces and ask her to fit them together again. Repeat with more pictures, this time cutting them into four pieces.

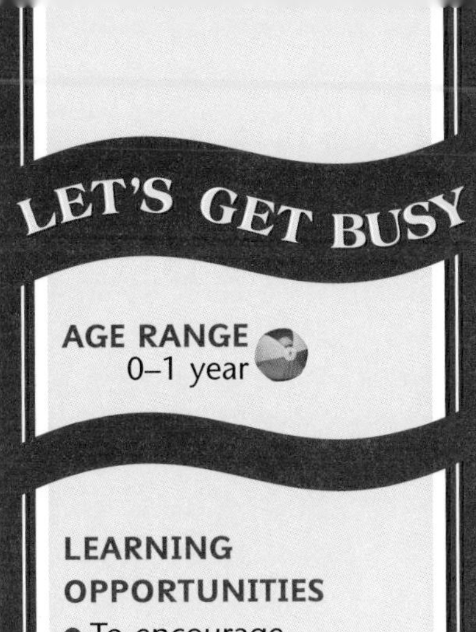

LEARNING OPPORTUNITIES

- To encourage recognition
- To develop hand–eye co-ordination
- To encourage object manipulation.

YOU WILL NEED

A small basket; set of family photographs; set of large wooden or plastic bricks; double-sided sticky tape; sticky-backed plastic; scissors.

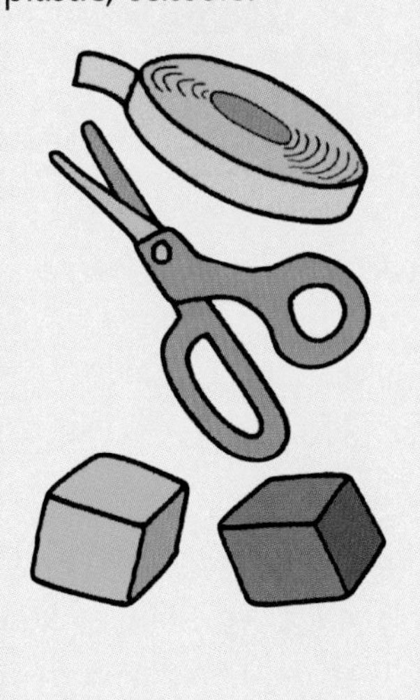

Find the face

Sharing the game

- Select a range of family photographs.
- Cut out a photo so that it fits one face of a brick. Stick the photo securely to the brick using sticky tape, and cover it with a piece of sticky-backed plastic.
- Make more 'photo-bricks' like this one. You may use more than one photo of the same person.
- Place the 'photo-bricks' in a small basket on the floor next to your baby. Let him explore the bricks, turning them in his hands to find a face.

- Say the name of the person that he finds, while pointing to the photograph.
- Offer him another brick, asking him to find the next face.
- Continue waiting and naming as your baby looks at more photographs.
- When your baby has looked at each brick, place them all in a line so that he can see them.

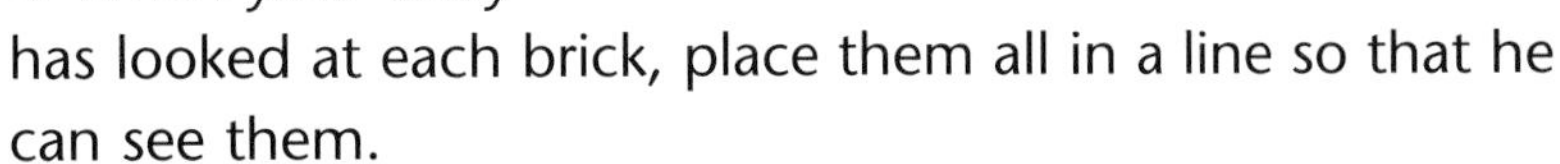

- Turn one of the bricks upside-down to hide the face. Watch to see if your baby tries to find the face again.

Taking it further

- Place the bricks in the basket and invite your baby to find the photograph of Mummy or Daddy. Wait for him to explore the bricks and find the appropriate photograph.
- Use pictures of animals or toys instead.

AGE RANGE
0–1 year

LEARNING OPPORTUNITIES
- To introduce a range of sounds
- To stimulate the senses
- To encourage exploration.

YOU WILL NEED
A needle and thread (adult use); range of brightly-coloured and patterned socks; large textured cushion; bells; crinkly paper; cotton-wool balls; lavender; ping-pong ball; small wooden brick; high chair.

THINK FIRST!
Make sure that the objects that you choose are suitable for your baby. Ensure that she does not place small objects into her mouth.

Pockets for the senses

Sharing the game

- Gather together a range of socks (odd ones are ideal!).
- Use your needle and thread to sew each sock securely to the cushion (some on each side of the cushion).
- Carefully select some suitable items to place into the socks. Try to choose a selection that will appeal to all your baby's senses. For example, for sound, place the bells; for smell, some lavender; for taste, an apple (beware of a choking risk); for touch, a small furry toy, and for sight, a highly-patterned item.
- Place a different item or group of items into each 'pocket'.
- Sit your baby in her high chair or on the floor beside you. Offer her the cushion to explore.
- Encourage her to pull and push at the socks, then to look inside a pocket by gently turning it inside out.
- As soon as your baby is eager to 'dig' into a sock to find the 'treasure', leave her to explore other socks, helping where necessary.

Taking it further

- Choose three cushions – one red, one blue and one yellow. Sew matching coloured socks on to the cushions and fill them with matching coloured items.

AGE RANGE
0–1 year

LEARNING OPPORTUNITIES
- To stimulate textural awareness
- To introduce colours
- To develop concentration skills.

YOU WILL NEED
Blue, red, yellow, green and patterned fabric in a variety of textures (such as cotton, velvet and felt); cushion or toy-animal stuffing; needle and thread (adult use); Velcro; scissors.

Padded chains

Sharing the game

- To play the game, you will need to make some coloured sets of padded shapes.
- Choose three pieces of blue fabric (such as cotton, velvet and felt). Cut out two discs from one fabric, two triangles from another and two squares from the third one. Sew the pairs of shapes together, leaving space for the stuffing to go in.
- Stuff the shapes and sew up the openings.
- Sew some Velcro to either end of each shape so that the shapes can be interlocked and joined to create a 'chain'.
- Now create red, yellow and green sets of shapes, using as many different fabrics as possible. Make another set from patterned material.
- Choose some of the shapes and join them, showing your baby what you are doing.
- Now let him play with the shapes. Demonstrate again how to join them together. Offer him two shapes and encourage him to copy you by joining them together in a chain.
- Encourage your baby to create a long chain and then, by demonstration, to take them apart.

Taking it further

- Join some bricks, such as Duplo, together. Encourage your baby to attempt to join two or three together.
- Offer your baby some lengths of fabric and encourage him to wrap them around his or your feet.
- Wrap some of the fabric around your knees and tie it, then around your wrist, telling your baby that because it is tied it doesn't fall off.

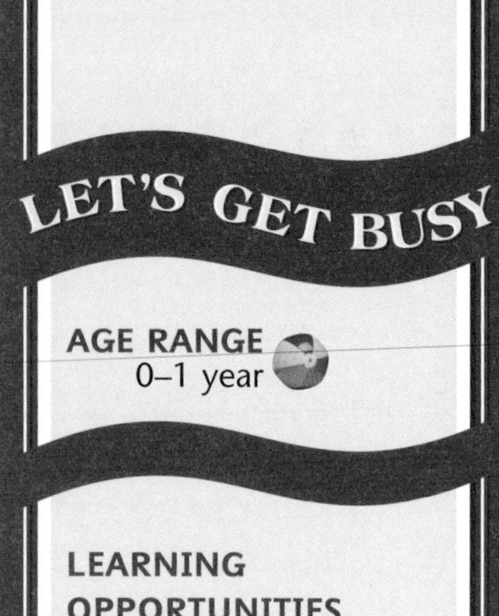

AGE RANGE
0–1 year

LEARNING OPPORTUNITIES
- To develop an awareness of objects
- To develop vocabulary
- To develop an interest in games.

YOU WILL NEED
A paddling pool or baby bath; four plastic containers with lids (such as clean, empty ice-cream tubs); ball; boat; small-world character; apple; four cushions; some of your baby's favourite toys.

Curiosity pool

Sharing the game

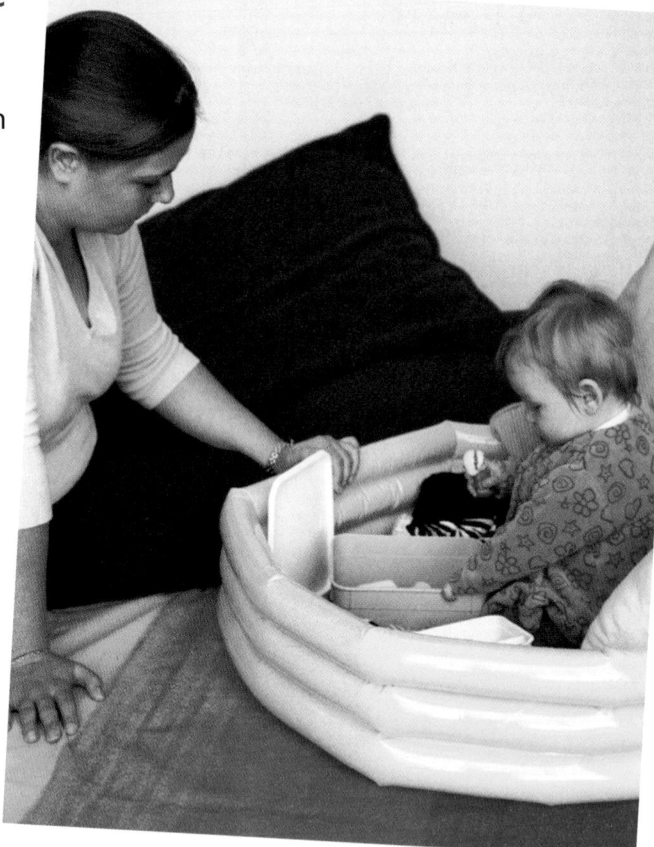

- Place the empty paddling pool on the floor (do not fill it with water!). Put the cushions, plastic containers and other items inside the pool.
- Sit your baby in the pool between all the resources and allow her to explore them.
- Hide a few of the items under the containers and cushions. Don't worry if your baby watches you.
- When they have all been hidden, allow your baby to 'find' them.
- Repeat the game as often as your baby wants you to! Each time, change the positions of the objects and challenge her to find them again.
- Each time your baby uncovers something, name it and describe it for her.
- Hide all the items again and encourage your baby to try to find a particular item.

Taking it further
- Take the paddling pool outside and remove the cushions. Place inside it various-sized containers with water in them and let your baby explore them.
- Develop your baby's vocabulary, using the words 'wet', 'dry', 'splash', 'float' and 'sink' when appropriate.

AGE RANGE
0–1 year

LEARNING OPPORTUNITIES
- To introduce the concept of raw and cooked foods
- To encourage exploration
- To develop an awareness of the sense of hearing.

YOU WILL NEED
A large plastic sheet; raw pasta; cooked pasta; two shallow bowls; two trays.

THINK FIRST!
Never leave your baby unattended with a plastic sheet. Also check that he does not have a gluten allergy before allowing him to taste the pasta. Make sure that he does not choke on small pieces of pasta – do not let him put the uncooked pasta into his mouth for risk of choking.

Hard and soft

Sharing the game

- Strip your baby down to his nappy and place him safely on the plastic sheet.
- Place the two bowls on either side of your baby. Put cooked pasta into one bowl and raw pasta into the other one.
- Start to explore the pasta with your hands, in the hope that your baby will copy you. If he doesn't, place a small amount of cooked pasta into his hand. Describe the pasta, using appropriate vocabulary such as 'soft', 'squashy' and 'stretchy'. Next, offer the raw pasta to your baby, again using appropriate description.
- While your baby is playing with the pasta, drop some raw pieces on to the tray. Describe the noise to him. Drop another piece and let him try too. Repeat the process with the cooked pasta on the other tray.
- Next, drop both kinds of pasta at the same time.
- Draw your baby's attention to the movement and sound.

Taking it further

- Show your baby how to put some pieces of cooked pasta into a plastic beaker. Then let him put some raw pasta into another beaker. Encourage him to shake the beakers and talk about the different noises that they make.

AGE RANGE
1–2 years

LEARNING OPPORTUNITIES
- To develop hand–eye co-ordination
- To encourage experimentation
- To develop an awareness of clothes.

YOU WILL NEED
Four small cushions; cardigan with poppers; small zipped jacket; trousers with buttons; small T-shirt; scraps of material; Velcro; needle and thread (adult use).

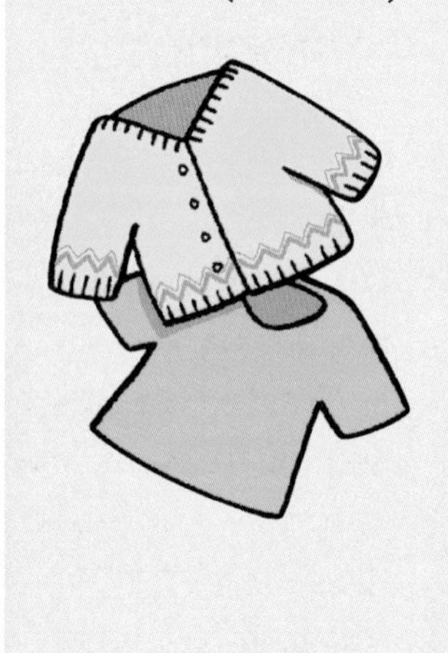

Do it up

Sharing the game

- Take one of the cushions and wrap the cardigan around it. Sew the cardigan on to the cushion, leaving the front panel loose so that your toddler can fasten and unfasten the poppers.
- Repeat this with another cushion and the small zipped jacket. Again, ensure that the jacket is securely sewn on to the cushion and that your toddler can use the zip.
- Attach the trousers to the third cushion. Secure them so that the legs are dangling! Make sure that your toddler can fasten and unfasten the buttons.
- Use a small T-shirt for the last cushion, use Velcro to attach a few flaps of material.
- Once all the cushions are ready, allow your toddler to interact freely with them at first. Watch what she does.
- Now offer her the cushions one at a time and let her attempt to do up the fastenings. Help her whenever necessary.

Taking it further

- Provide a range of clothing with a variety of fastenings. Offer the clothes to your toddler. Let her attempt to fasten and unfasten them. Offer support if it is needed. Play alongside your child to help her to explore the clothing fully.

AGE RANGE
1–2 years

LEARNING OPPORTUNITIES
- To encourage exploration
- To develop new vocabulary
- To encourage making choices.

YOU WILL NEED
A mug tree; fir cone; large shiny ball; sparkly hairslide; spinning top; length of ribbon; large semi-precious stone; five or six small cotton or muslin bags (large enough for your toddler to put his hand in).

Bags of treasure

Sharing the game

- Place one of the items in each of the cotton or muslin bags. Items that are very different from one another are ideal. The items mentioned in 'You will need' are only suggestions.
- Hang each of the filled bags on to the mug tree.
- Now place the mug tree on the floor next to your toddler. Sit beside him and encourage him to choose a bag.
- Offer your toddler some help to open the bags if necessary. As far as possible, leave him to discover the treasure for himself.
- Allow your toddler to explore each new discovery. Encourage him to find out a use for the object, or let him make up a game with it (such as putting it inside a box, or dancing with it!). If he cannot find a use for it, demonstrate a suggestion for him to copy.
- Name each item that your toddler removes from a bag.

- At the end of the game, encourage your toddler to place the items back into the bags and hook them on to the mug tree.

Taking it further

- Change all the items in the bags on a regular basis.
- Create two identical sets of treasure. Place one set of treasure in the bags and the other in a small basket. Invite your toddler to choose an item from a bag and encourage him to find the matching item from the box.

LET'S GET BUSY

AGE RANGE
1–2 years

LEARNING OPPORTUNITIES
- To introduce the concept of large and small
- To challenge manipulative skills
- To encourage listening and watching.

YOU WILL NEED
A set of nesting cups; nesting doll; set of nesting boxes; range of plastic tubs; large piece of fabric or playmat.

Cups to nest

Sharing the game

- Roll out the piece of fabric (or playmat) in a comfortable area.
- Place the nesting cups, doll, boxes and tubs on to the fabric.
- Sit down with the equipment and invite your toddler to join you. Let her explore each of the sets of nests.
- Choose a small doll and place it inside one of the boxes.
- Use appropriate vocabulary and body language to pretend that you have lost the doll.
- Repeat the game, varying the way that you hide the objects. For example, hide a small box inside a large doll under a large plastic tub!
- Now concentrate on one of the nesting sets, such as the dolls. Gather all the dolls together and help your toddler to place them, one inside the other, to complete the set. Support your toddler while she tries the activity herself.
- Repeat with each set of nests.

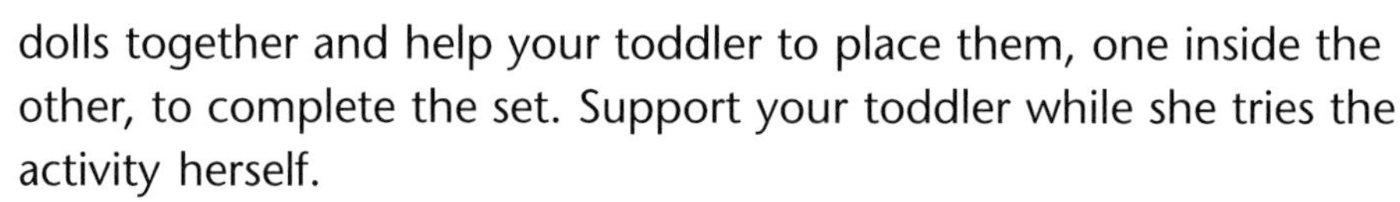

Taking it further

- Invite your toddler to show you the smallest doll, the largest box and so on.
- Ask her to place the biggest plastic box on the floor and to put the little doll inside. Can she then put the big doll in the small box?
- Introduce other sets of objects that have a range of sizes for your toddler to explore and compare.

AGE RANGE
1–2 years

LEARNING OPPORTUNITIES
- To stimulate natural curiosity
- To develop familiarity with objects
- To copy movements.

YOU WILL NEED
A large box; string or wool; cotton wool; foil; tissue; ribbons; cardboard strips; small-world people; fir cones.

THINK FIRST!
Do not let your toddler put small objects into her mouth for risk of choking. Also, always supervise her when she is using string, wool, ribbons and so on.

Bits and bobs

Sharing the game

- Make some interesting objects for your toddler to explore, such as a small-world person wrapped in foil, a fir cone wrapped in tissue and tied up with string, and a ribbon wrapped around a cardboard strip. Place these objects and the other items into the large box.
- Sit with your child, next to the box. Encourage her to explore the items. Choose one of the special objects that you have already created and look at it closely together.
- Offer it to your toddler and tap parts of it, naming them. Let her explore the whole object.
- Choose some of the items and slowly join them together. Describe what you are doing and tell your toddler to look at the object that you have made.
- Now offer your toddler a selection of objects and help her to join them together in some way. Let her take the lead, if she wishes, and offer her help when she needs it. Encourage her to practise wrapping, rolling, tying and unwrapping.

Taking it further

- Choose each item, one at a time. Slowly unravel the string, wool and rolled-up ribbons. Show your toddler what you are doing and encourage her to copy you.
- Lay out some of the objects, such as a length of ribbon next to an unrolled length of string, next to some silver foil and flattened-out tissue paper. Invite your toddler to mix, scrunch and roll the items.

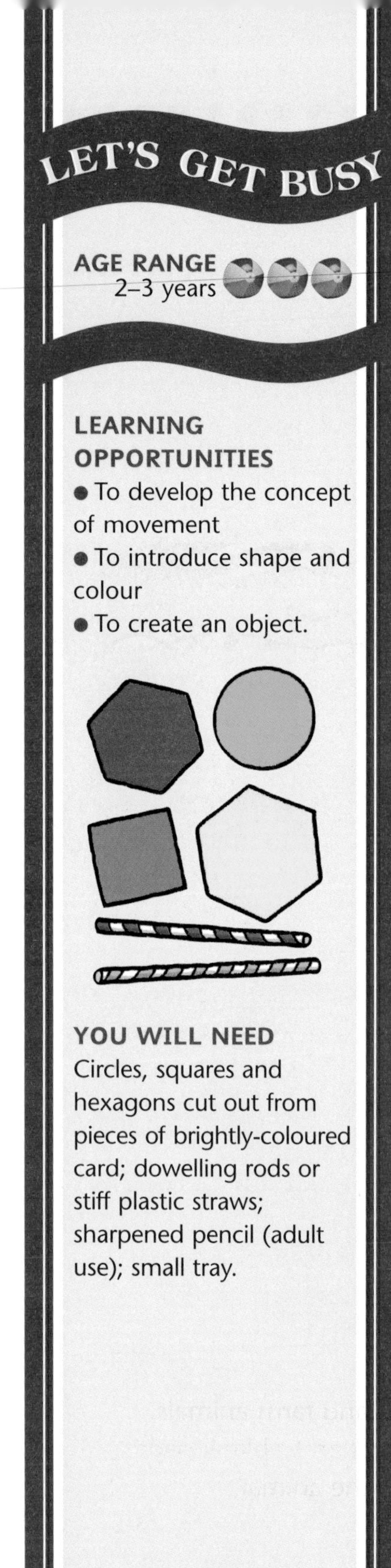

LET'S GET BUSY

AGE RANGE
2–3 years

LEARNING OPPORTUNITIES

- To develop the concept of movement
- To introduce shape and colour
- To create an object.

YOU WILL NEED

Circles, squares and hexagons cut out from pieces of brightly-coloured card; dowelling rods or stiff plastic straws; sharpened pencil (adult use); small tray.

Spin it around

Sharing the game

- Make a hole in the middle of each shape using a sharpened pencil. Ensure that the holes are big enough to push a dowelling rod or straw through.
- Place the shapes into a small tray and put the dowelling rods or straws next to the tray.
- Invite your child to look at and explore the shapes. For each shape that he chooses, tell him its name and colour.
- Choose one of the shapes and challenge your child to find a matching one.
- Next, encourage him to identify a shape by name, then by colour. When he is ready, ask him to find specific shapes such as a blue triangle, a red circle and so on.
- Demonstrate how to push a dowelling rod or straw through one of the shapes. Encourage your child to copy you.
- Attempt to spin the shapes around.

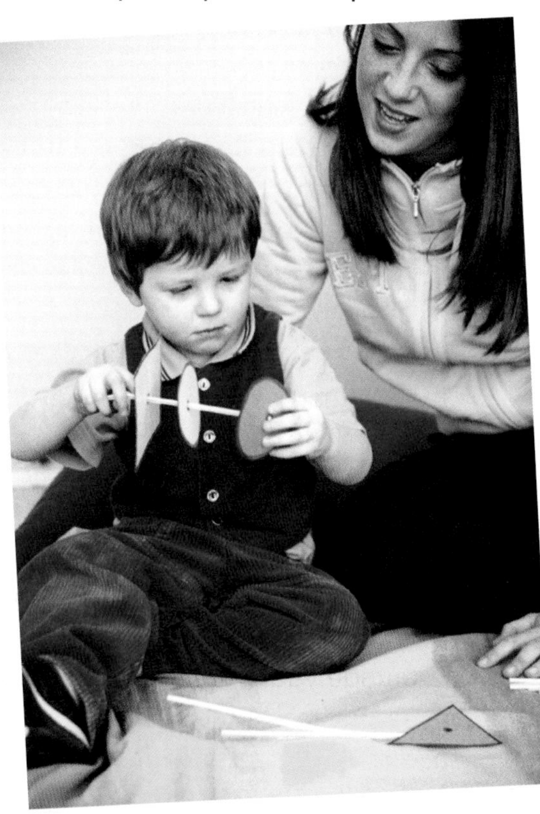

- Place a variety of shapes in different colours on to your straw, naming the colour and shape each time.
- Encourage your child to 'copy' naming the shapes and colours if he can.

Taking it further

- Continue the spinning theme by encouraging your child to spin around or to play with a spinning top.
- Look at examples of spinning in everyday life, such as ingredients being mixed and spun around in a bowl; car wheels spinning; the washing machine spinning, and so on.

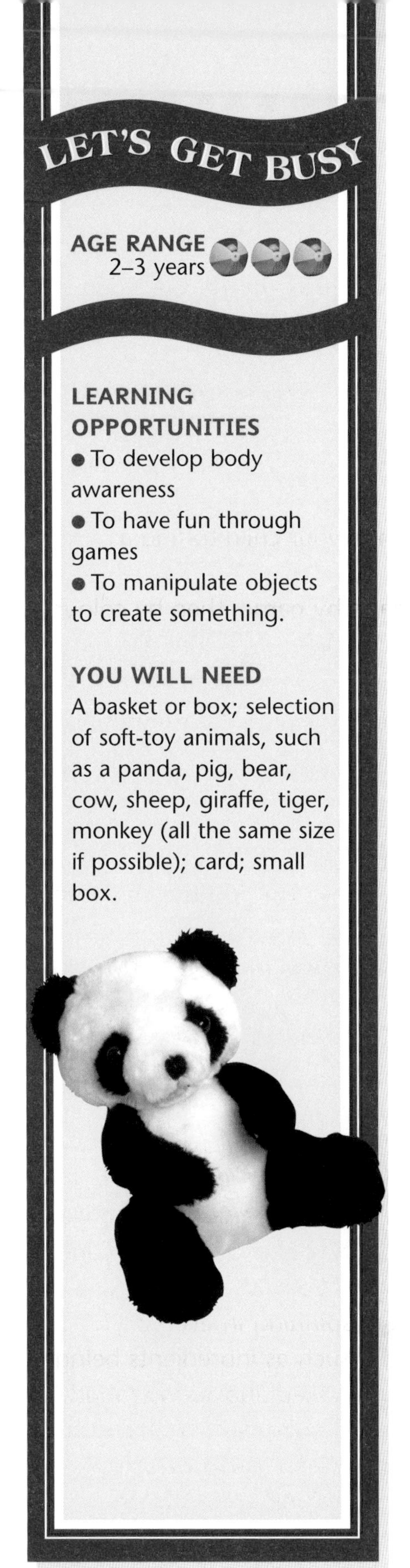

AGE RANGE
2–3 years

LEARNING OPPORTUNITIES
- To develop body awareness
- To have fun through games
- To manipulate objects to create something.

YOU WILL NEED
A basket or box; selection of soft-toy animals, such as a panda, pig, bear, cow, sheep, giraffe, tiger, monkey (all the same size if possible); card; small box.

Animal parts

Sharing the game

- Create a set of animal cards, representing the range of soft toys that you have. The drawings need only be very basic. If preferred, use a colouring book to cut the pictures from.
- Cut the finished animal cards into two pieces (head and body) and place all the cards inside a small box.
- Take each soft toy and place it in a basket or box. Invite your child to choose one of the toys. Ask her to name it, then make the animal sound with you. Discuss the animal and its colour, shape and form.
- Now show your child the animal cards. Explain that she needs to find the two parts of the animal – its head and its body. Can she match any of the cards together? Help her to match the cards for each animal.
- Now match the animal cards with the soft toys. Encourage her to help you.
- Mix some of the animals up and challenge your child to tell you what is not right. Can she correct your mistake?

Taking it further

- Make different animal sets, such as pets and farm animals.
- Use some Blu-Tack to stick the head cards on to blank paper. Encourage your child to draw the body of the animal.
- Use Blu-Tack to stick a body card on to a piece of paper. Invite your child to make up some fun animals by trying out different head cards with the body!

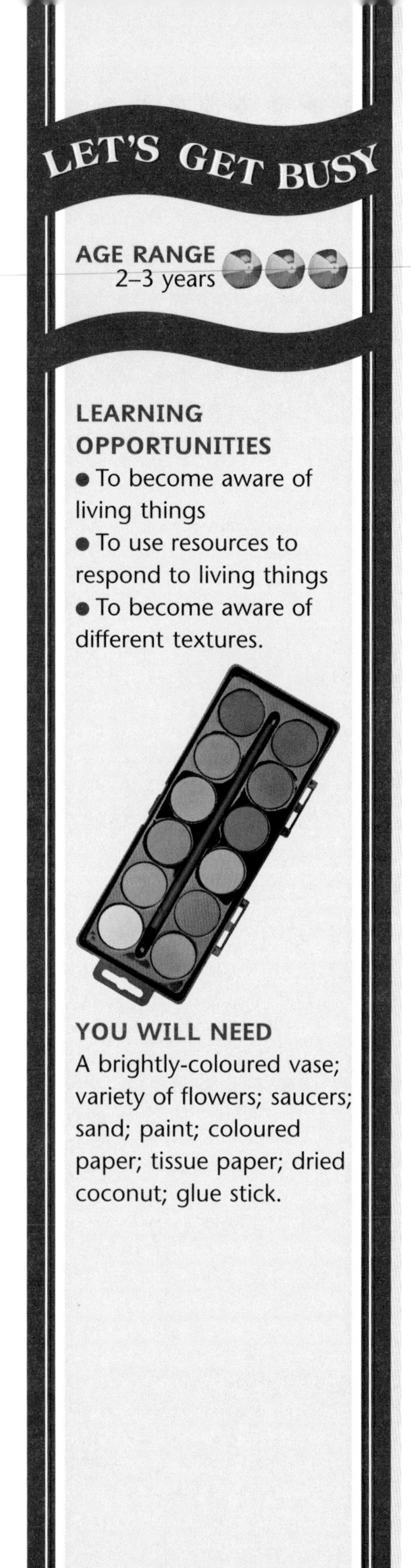

LET'S GET BUSY

AGE RANGE
2–3 years

LEARNING OPPORTUNITIES

- To become aware of living things
- To use resources to respond to living things
- To become aware of different textures.

YOU WILL NEED

A brightly-coloured vase; variety of flowers; saucers; sand; paint; coloured paper; tissue paper; dried coconut; glue stick.

Stick it on

Sharing the game

- Look at the flowers with your child. Talk about each one, naming them if possible.
- Ask your child what his favourite flower is. Can he find the pink one, the yellow one and so on?
- Put some water in the vase and invite your child to choose one flower at a time and place it in the vase. Talk about the arrangement together.
- Place all the items on to the saucers. Ask your child if he would like to use the materials to make a flower picture.
- Create a picture alongside your child. Encourage him to watch what you are doing and invite him to try some of your ideas. Show him how to use a glue stick sparingly and how to scatter a little coconut or sand on to the glue to make a textured pattern.
- Invite your child to help you to rip the coloured and tissue paper into little pieces. Use the paper to put the finishing touches to your flower pictures.

Taking it further

- Make an animal picture together. Show your child some animal pictures to stimulate his imagination. Provide him with animal-print designed paper and other items that reflect the colours and textures of a range of animals.

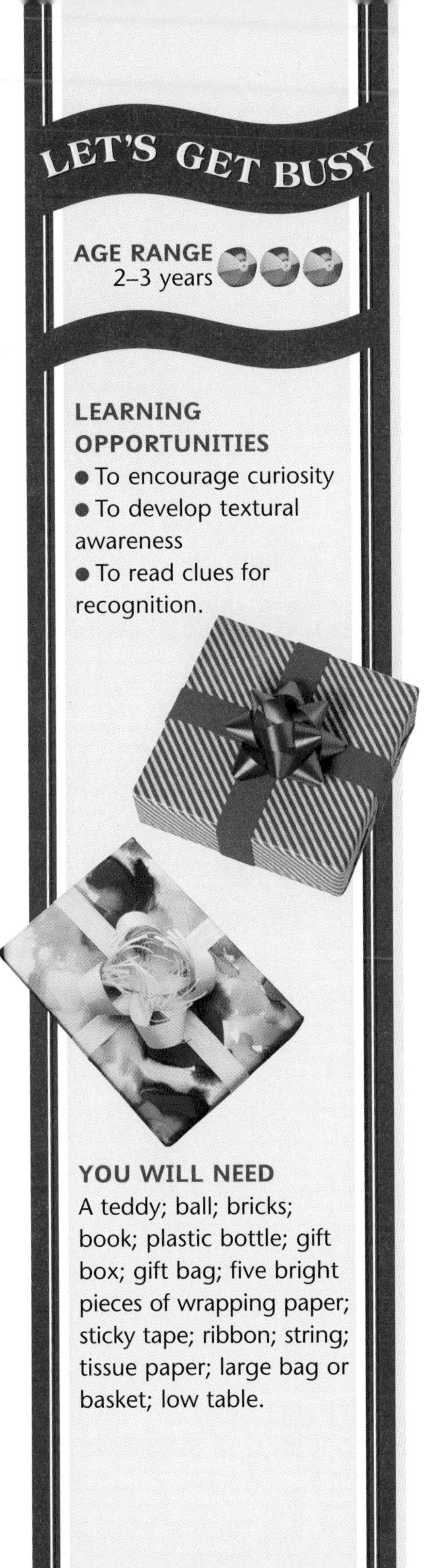

LET'S GET BUSY

AGE RANGE
2–3 years

LEARNING OPPORTUNITIES
- To encourage curiosity
- To develop textural awareness
- To read clues for recognition.

YOU WILL NEED
A teddy; ball; bricks; book; plastic bottle; gift box; gift bag; five bright pieces of wrapping paper; sticky tape; ribbon; string; tissue paper; large bag or basket; low table.

Unwrap the parcels

Sharing the game

- Wrap each item in a different type of wrapping before presenting any to your child. Place the bricks inside the gift box and the plastic bottle inside the gift bag, and wrap the other objects in the paper, using sticky tape for one, ribbon for another and string for the last one. Try to match the colour of the contents with the paper, box or bag.
- Place the wrapped items in a large bag or basket.
- Encourage your child to help you lift the bag (or basket) and bring it to a low table or floor space.
- Invite your child to take one parcel out and ask her what colour it is. What does she think is inside?
- Encourage your child to shake and squeeze it. Invite her to guess what it might be.
- Ask her to describe what she feels and hears.
- Now invite your child to rip off a little of the wrapping to give her a clue. Let her continue to rip it, a little at a time, until she guesses correctly or until she has unwrapped the whole parcel.
- Repeat with each parcel. Remember to encourage your toddler to undo the ties herself and to make as many guesses as she likes.

Taking it further

- Choose a few items from around the house and wrap them with your child. If possible, present them to someone else to do the guessing and the unwrapping.

LET'S GET BUSY

AGE RANGE
2–3 years

LEARNING OPPORTUNITIES
- To encourage an awareness of movement
- To encourage an awareness of colour
- To introduce the concept of light and reflection.

YOU WILL NEED
Three torches of different sizes; thin transparent paper in different colours; sticky tape; large blank wall space.

Light reflection

Sharing the game

- Sit on the floor near to the wall space. Give your child the torches and let him explore them.
- Encourage him to direct the torch beams around the wall, on his body, feet and hands, and then on you.
- Take a torch and demonstrate moving the beam up and down on the wall space a few times. Invite your child to copy your movements.
- Play the light from side to side. Invite your child to copy.
- Make circles and zigzags with the torch beam.
- Now invite your child to take the lead, making the patterns for you to copy.
- Exclaim that some of his patterns were too hard and ask him to show you again! Ask him if you followed his patterns correctly.
- Offer pieces of thin transparent coloured paper to your child, helping him to tape one that he likes to his torch. Repeat some of the patterns in the new colour. Continue the activity using the three torches and the different colours.

Taking it further

- Use ink markers to create patterns or simple shapes on the coloured paper. Ideas include a fish, smiling face or flower. Shine the torch and see your child's amazement at the pictures appearing on the wall.
- Continue to make different pictures and challenge your child to guess what they are. Let him create 'pictures' for you to guess.

CHAPTER 7

TOGETHER TIME

The activities in this chapter, as well as providing plenty of fun opportunities, can be used as the basis for some important listening and responding work with your child. They have been intended as play-based activities, but will also make your time together purposeful and interesting.

TOGETHER TIME

Key to the health and well-being of any baby, toddler or young child is the building of strong relationships with their parents and carers. Naturally, the essential ingredient to build these relationships is time spent together. The character of this time when concentrating on 'being together' can vary enormously – it can be relaxed and quiet, or busy and focused.

The activities in this chapter have been designed to encourage development in many areas, but particularly in communication and language, skills that are essential to establishing deep and lasting bonds.

One of the first things that a parent does when they are presented with a new baby is to hold her close and speak softly to 'introduce' themselves. When you are speaking to a very young child, the tone of your voice is automatically soft and comforting. A baby will also give an automatic response to your voice – even a very young baby will turn to the sound of her mother's voice.

How you can help

- When pushing your child in her pram or buggy, talk to her about what you are passing, what you are wearing and what is hanging on the pram/buggy.
- When dressing your child, talk about the clothes that you are taking off and those that you are putting on her.
- Involve her in as much of your day as you can, without smothering her. Remember that she needs her own space and time to explore on her own.

COMMUNICATION

In the first year of her life, a baby's communication skills quickly develop from simply crying to indicate hunger, boredom or another need, to simple 'baby talk'. The 'coo' and 'goo' sounds take on more and more complexity as she develops, and you will hear your baby 'talking' to her toys and to you. The more you talk to your baby, the more information

she has available to her to imitate with her own 'speech'.

Talking to your baby will help her to develop her skills and confidence to respond. During any routine activity, it is beneficial to 'chat' to your baby. The content is less important than the nature of the words – always try to use proper words rather than baby talk.

Around six months of age, you may notice that your baby's responses become less random; she is beginning to recognise and understand the language that you use. It is likely that she will be confident in imitating some of the sounds that she hears.

How you can help

- Play little talking games while you are busy cleaning. If your child is watching you, try to initiate conversation by asking her questions.
- As she 'talks' to you, repeat what she says (pretend to understand, making suggestions as to what she is saying).
- Gather a variety of sound makers and sit with your child. Create a sound, then use words to describe it. Try to imitate the noise that you have made and encourage your child to do the same.
- Look through different magazines together. Your child will enjoy looking at the pictures with you and will delight in the intimacy of the experience. Draw her attention to the various photographs on the pages.
- Share lots of books with your child. Do not be concerned with the story, just focus on the pictures, using simple vocabulary to describe them.

WORDS, WORDS, WORDS

When your child begins to use real words, there is a considerable jump in the level of shared understanding between you and her. As the range of vocabulary increases, not only does the level of understanding increase, but your child will also become more involved in the communication process.

Singing and talking together, and listening attentively to your child, will encourage her vocabulary to expand. While your toddler has a handful of words that she can use and understand, she will also continue to use some of her baby language. Keep up the habit of talking to her and encourage her to listen – her vocabulary will continue to grow. By her second birthday, your toddler will be able to make herself very well understood – naming toys, body parts and many other items to which she has been introduced. By the age of three, she will have the confidence to use over one thousand words and her conversation and turn of phrase will provide many laughs and moments of happiness!

How you can help

- Play a copying game. Explain to your child that you have a pile of toys and that as you hold up a toy you would like her to name it
- Set the table and sit at it with your child. Invite her to point to the cup, plate, mat and so on. Then ask her to name items that you point to.
- Go to a shop, not to buy anything, but to encourage your child to talk about what she can see. Help her to expand her vocabulary.
- Take your child to the park. Invite her to hop, skip, jump, slide and swing. As she carries out each instruction, she is showing her understanding. Make some movements yourself and invite her to describe them.

AGE RANGE
0–1 year

LEARNING OPPORTUNITIES
- To introduce new vocabulary
- To encourage exploration during water play
- To encourage fun in a daily routine.

YOU WILL NEED
A bath or paddling pool; bubble bath; sponge; soap; rubber duck; towel; dry clothes or pyjamas; toothbrush; picture word book showing pictures of bathtime or water play.

THINK FIRST!
Children with eczema must use special oils in the bath. Make sure that your baby does not have sensitive skin before using soap or bubble bath.

Water play

Sharing the game

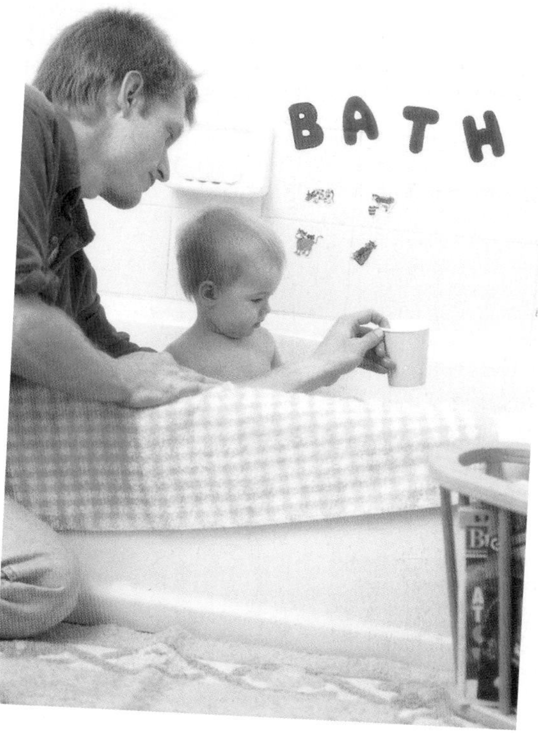

- Before putting your child in the bath or before playing in a paddling pool, look at some pictures of bathtime or water-play objects and activities. Talk about what you can see together.
- When you have checked that the water temperature is suitable, place your baby in the water.
- Let her splash around for a few minutes. Put the duck in the water and invite your baby to move it around. Allow her to play with it for a few more minutes.
- Next, add some baby bubble bath and encourage your baby to splash, creating lots of bubbles.
- Hand her the duck and some soap. Gently rub the soap on the duck, then on her.
- Squeeze out a sponge and let the water dribble on to your baby to clear the soap from her skin. Each time you do something new, describe what is happening.
- When your baby is ready, wrap her in a towel. Put on her clothes (or pyjamas) and look at the picture books again.

Taking it further

- Create a set of photographs depicting the routine of washing hands and face. Talk about the pictures together.
- Add other sets to your series, such as a set for eating breakfast or for getting dressed.
- Look at the photographs from time to time and use them to inspire some role-play games by acting out the actions shown.

TOGETHER TIME

AGE RANGE
0–1 year

LEARNING OPPORTUNITIES
- To explore features of our world
- To develop hand–eye co-ordination
- To encourage watching and imitation.

YOU WILL NEED
A light-coloured cushion; green fabric paint; six or seven silk flower heads; Velcro; glue; vase of fresh flowers.

Flower cushion

Sharing the game

- Offer your baby a few silk flowers to explore.
- Cut the flower heads from the stems and glue a small piece of Velcro on to the back of each one.
- Place the flower heads in a small pile on the floor where your baby can play with them. If he sometimes uses a walker with a tray, then place them on his tray.
- Use the fabric paint to paint three or four stems on to the cushion. Draw your baby's attention to what you are doing and encourage him to watch you.

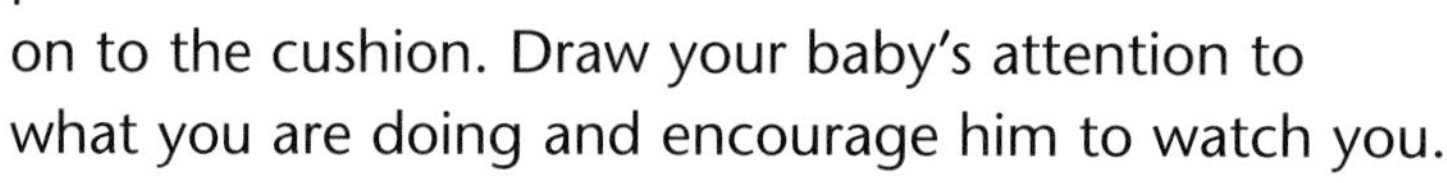

- Once the paint is dry, encourage your baby to watch while you 'trace' your finger along each of the stems. Now hold your baby's finger and trace it along the stems too.
- Attach a small piece of Velcro to the top of each painted stem.
- Now let your baby touch some of the real flowers. Describe them to him as he touches them.
- Once the cushion is dry, take one silk flower head at a time and attach it to the cushion.
- When all the flower heads are placed, offer the cushion to your baby, encouraging him to take the heads off by pulling at the Velcro.
- Show your baby how to stick them on again to create the bunch of flowers. Repeat this a few times, encouraging your baby to try to do this by himself.

Taking it further

- Paint a circle (the sun) on to another cushion. Make some material stripes (the rays) that can be added and removed by attaching Velcro.
- Alternatively, paint a face on a cushion and make some Velcro features to add and remove!

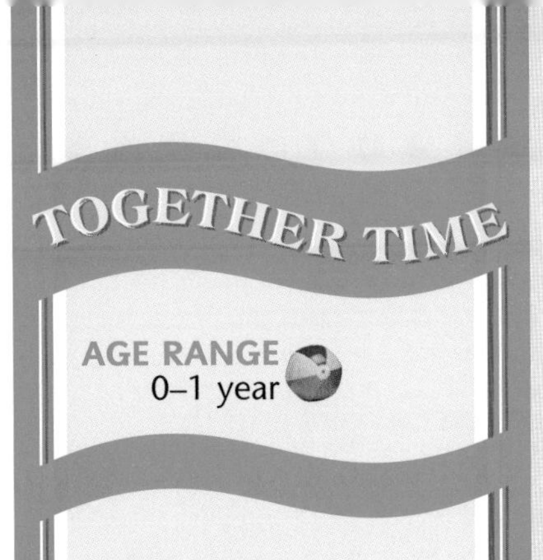

AGE RANGE
0–1 year

LEARNING OPPORTUNITIES
- To encourage manipulation
- To encourage matching skills
- To explore animals by markings and names.

YOU WILL NEED
A pop-up toy featuring farm animals or sea creatures, suitable for babies; set of toy animals to match the pop-up animals; cushion.

Pop-up look

Sharing the game

- Sit beside your baby and use a cushion to play 'Peek-a-boo'. Then hide behind a chair or table and continue to 'pop out'.
- Now sit with your baby on the floor and place the pop-up toy in front of her.

- Show your baby how to use the toy and encourage her to push, pull or twist the buttons to make the animals pop up. Each time an animal pops up, say its name, then push it back down, exclaiming, 'Oh, it's gone!'.
- Pop up all the animals and ask your baby to try to push them down again.

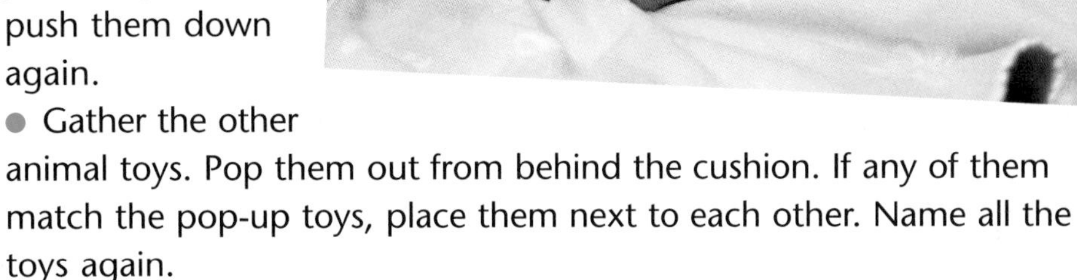

- Gather the other animal toys. Pop them out from behind the cushion. If any of them match the pop-up toys, place them next to each other. Name all the toys again.
- Hold one of the little toys in your hand and push it into your fist so that it is hidden from view. Repeat with several of the other animals.
- Challenge your baby to find (or pop up) an animal that you ask for. Can she name the animal or make its sound (such as 'baa')?

Taking it further

- Look through a picture book with simple animal pictures inside. Do any of the animals in the book match the animals that you have been playing with? Help your baby to match a toy animal with an animal in the book.

AGE RANGE
0–1 year

LEARNING OPPORTUNITIES
- To support natural curiosity
- To encourage exploration
- To develop a sense of colour.

YOU WILL NEED
A selection of different-coloured beakers; variety of items small enough to fit underneath or inside the beakers (the same colours as the beakers); large box.

Hide under beakers

Sharing the game

- Sit on the floor beside your baby. Place the beakers and the matching coloured items into the large box, then put the box next to your baby.
- Take out a large beaker and place it on the floor. Select an item of the same colour (for example, a small yellow toy duck for a yellow beaker) and place it inside the beaker.
- Repeat this with a second item and beaker – for example, put a blue sock inside a blue beaker.
- Now choose a third item and place it on the floor next to the matching beaker (for example, a red beaker and a red plastic spoon). Watch to see if your baby places the spoon inside the red beaker. (Remember, it is not important if he gets it wrong – it is the doing or trying which is important.)
- Continue to put the beakers down next to your baby and to place matching coloured items near to them, and see if your baby tries to put the items inside.

Taking it further

- Clean the beakers and hide some finger foods underneath them at snack time. Use this as a game to encourage your baby to try finger foods that he does not normally like.

AGE RANGE
0–1 year

LEARNING OPPORTUNITIES

- To encourage manipulation of objects
- To encourage listening and concentration
- To introduce new vocabulary.

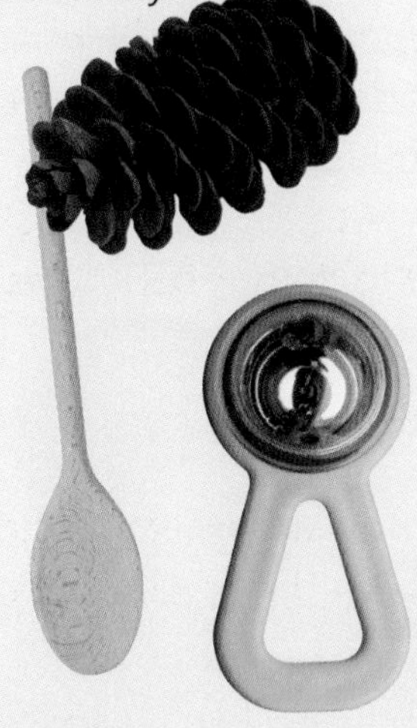

YOU WILL NEED

A selection of everyday items (as wide a variety of shapes, sizes and textures as possible). Some of the items should be easy to pick up and others should be more difficult.

What can I hold?

Sharing the game

- Place items such as a rattle, a wooden spoon, a metal bowl, a large fir cone, a furry toy animal, a small ball, a scoop and a small bucket on the floor.
- Sit beside your baby and encourage her to explore each of the items.
- As your baby picks up an item, name it and describe it using one or two words. Invite her to choose another item, and again name it and describe it.
- Ask your baby questions as she attempts to grasp and hold each item, for example, 'Does it make a noise?', 'Is it soft?' and so on.

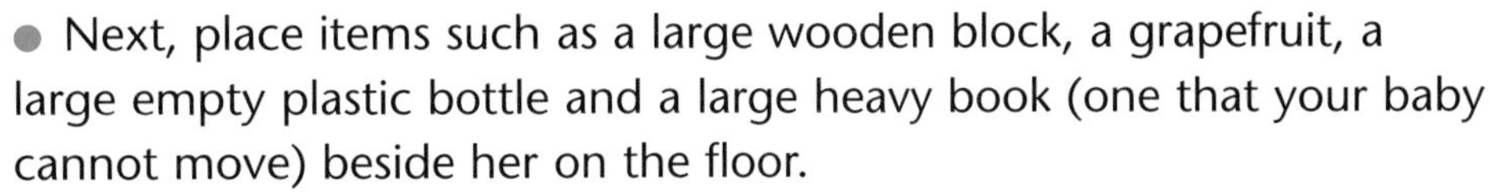

- Next, place items such as a large wooden block, a grapefruit, a large empty plastic bottle and a large heavy book (one that your baby cannot move) beside her on the floor.
- Pick each item up and then place it back down, so that she is encouraged to try lifting them.
- Help your baby to lift the items, inviting her to use both hands. Talk about how heavy the objects are and make dramatic gestures to indicate that they are hard to pick up!

Taking it further

- Put a wet cloth, a wet bar of soap and a sticky spoon inside a bowl. Encourage your baby to pick up the objects. Use appropriate language to describe what she is touching.

AGE RANGE
1–2 years

LEARNING OPPORTUNITIES
- To encourage an awareness of the home environment
- To explore household objects
- To develop a sense of fun.

YOU WILL NEED
Five or six favourite toys.

Where's my toy?

Sharing the game

- While your toddler is asleep or is interacting with another adult, place the toys around the house or nursery. Place them where they would not normally be found.
- Sit with your toddler on your knee and describe the room where you are. Name it and a few of the items normally found in it. Suggest that you go on a 'journey' to find some 'treasure'!
- Take your toddler for a walk around your house or nursery. As you enter each room, name it and describe it a little. For example, say, 'Oh, look, the dining room! This is where we have our meals. Look, there is Sue's chair. Oh, what's this? It looks like a little blue animal. It has two big ears and a long trunk. Is Nellie your favourite elephant?'.
- Name and describe the things that your toddler approaches in each room. If he does not show much interest in the game, draw his attention to a few pictures or special ornaments.
- Encourage him to name his toy when he comes across it. Praise him whenever he expresses himself through language or body movements.

Taking it further

- Place your toddler's favourite toys in a bag or box. Give it to your toddler and encourage him to help you to hide the toys, one in each room. Then return to where you started and gather them all in! Challenge your toddler to remember where he hid them.

AGE RANGE
1–2 years

LEARNING OPPORTUNITIES

- To stimulate natural curiosity
- To develop the sense of touch
- To introduce the idea of changing an object by manipulation (for example, by ripping).

YOU WILL NEED

A large box with a lid; tissue paper; crêpe paper; silver foil; corrugated paper; crinkly paper; cotton wool; bubble wrap.

THINK FIRST!
Take care to avoid paper cuts when rubbing the papers on to hands and feet.

Box of paper

Sharing the game

- Place the various materials (of different textures, lengths and colours) inside the box and close the lid.
- Invite your toddler to sit next to you and beside the box.
- Encourage her to guess what is inside the box. Can she help you to shake it a little?
- Open the lid slightly and ask her to peek inside. Can she see anything? What could she bring out? Encourage her to pull out one of the items from the box. If your toddler is reluctant to do this, try pulling out a small corner of an item and encouraging her to pull out the rest.

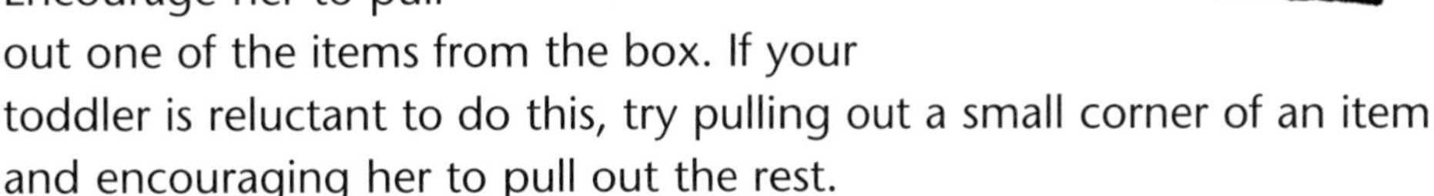

- Repeat this a few times, then take the lid off. Allow your toddler to explore the contents freely.

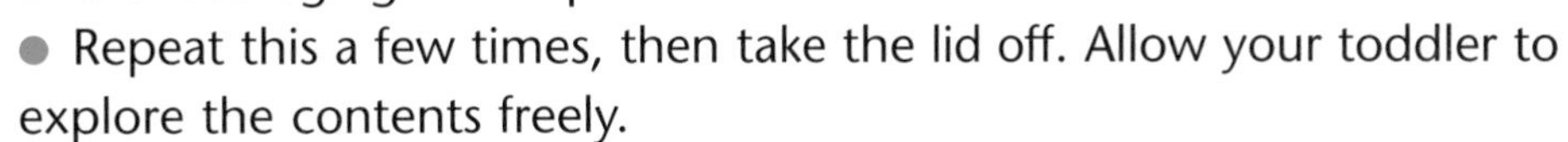

- Now invite her to rub an item between her palms, on her cheeks, then on your cheeks.
- Next, take off both your own shoes and your toddler's. Gently rub the different pieces on to both sets of feet!
- Put the items on the floor and walk around on top of them together. Stop and make ruffling noises with your feet.

Taking it further

- After exploring the various items, rip a small piece off one of them, then encourage your toddler to rip another.
- Rip more items off, then glue a variety of ripped pieces on to the box to decorate it.

Rolling over

Sharing the game

- Having gathered together a selection of bottles, part-fill a clear one with pennies, another with tinsel and a third with bubble bath. Screw on the lids tightly.
- Sit on the floor with your toddler and describe each bottle and its contents, as he explores them.
- Choose one of the bottles, place it in front of you and gently rock it back and forth in front of you. Encourage your toddler to sit down and try this with another bottle.
- While he copies your movements, let your bottle slowly roll a little too far and exclaim in response.
- Retrieve your bottle and repeat, this time pushing the bottle away. Invite your toddler to try this too. Repeat a few times.
- Take the other three bottles and have one with sand, one with sequins or glitter, and one empty.
- Sit opposite your toddler and roll the bottles to him, one at a time. Encourage him to push them back to you. See how far you can roll each bottle.
- Now try spinning the bottles around beside you.
- Next, stand the bottles up and encourage him to knock them over. Try to describe the sounds as they roll and fall.

Taking it further

- Decorate an old box. Select four opaque bottles and fill three of them with water, sand and feathers, leaving the fourth one empty, so that each is a different weight. Encourage your toddler to lift each bottle in turn and place it in the box.

LEARNING OPPORTUNITIES

- To develop gross motor skills
- To encourage co-ordination skills
- To develop a sense of movement.

YOU WILL NEED

Six clear plastic bottles with lids (one- or two-litre size); items to put inside, such as pennies, tinsel, bubble bath, sand and sequins.

THINK FIRST! Make sure that your toddler does not put small items into his mouth for risk of choking.

AGE RANGE
1–2 years

LEARNING OPPORTUNITIES
- To develop an awareness of language
- To develop an awareness of rhythm and rhyme
- To introduce positional language.

YOU WILL NEED
Six toys that relate to rhymes that your toddler is familiar with; six pictures (approximately A4 size) of a car, horse, train, bicycle, chair and boat; brightly-coloured pillowcase.

Sing along

Sharing the game

- Place all the items inside the pillowcase.
- Sit on the floor with your toddler and take out the pictures.
- Show the pictures one at a time, encouraging your toddler to name the item in the picture. Place all the pictures spaced out on the floor.
- Invite your toddler to remove one of the toys from the pillowcase (for example, a toy mouse). Sing 'Hickory Dickory Dock' (Traditional), or whichever rhyme relates to the toy that your child has chosen.
- As you sing the song, make the toy dance around in time to the tune, then hand it to your toddler.
- Add an extra line to the end of the song, for example:

  ...the clock struck one,
  the mouse ran down,
  Hickory Dickory Dock,
  Tick tock...
  ...and then the mouse jumped in the car!
- Encourage your child to put the mouse on the picture of the car.
- Repeat the rhyme, this time stopping on the train, and so on.
- Play the game again with a different toy animal and rhyme – for example, a rabbit for 'Little Peter Rabbit', a dog for 'How Much is That Doggie in the Window?' and a spider for 'Incy Wincy Spider', all from *This Little Puffin...* compiled by Elizabeth Matterson (Puffin Books).

Taking it further

- Sing a rhyme and invite your toddler to choose a picture for the animal to hide under.
- When all the songs have been sung and the animals have been hidden, challenge your toddler to find the mouse, the spider and so on.

AGE RANGE
1–2 years

LEARNING OPPORTUNITIES
- To encourage response to music
- To develop concentration and listening skills
- To develop understanding of movement.

YOU WILL NEED
A tape recorder; tape with a variety of short extracts of music; story-books or photographs depicting young children stretching, exercising and dancing.

Movement to music

Sharing the game

- Sit or lie on the floor beside your toddler and look at the books together. Have the music playing in the background.
- Now listen more carefully to the music and talk to your toddler about it. Make comments and ask him questions, for example, 'Can you hear the soft quiet music?', 'Can you hear the trumpet playing?', 'Oh, that's the drums!' and so on.
- When the tempo changes, tap your fingers on the floor and encourage your toddler to join in.
- Then gently tap your whole hand on the floor. Sit up and gently tap your toes, then your whole foot. Invite your toddler to copy you.
- When the tempo changes again, go on to your knees and bob up and down, or sway from side to side. Tap your hands on the sides of your legs and on your knees.
- Next, stand up, walking backwards and forwards in time to the music, encouraging your toddler to copy you.
- Each time you move, use appropriate language to describe the movement and show your toddler how to do it.
- Now try standing opposite your toddler and holding hands. Move around in a circle and back again.

Taking it further

- Rather than taped music, use a drum, whistle, tambourine or bells to create a rhythm for yourself and your toddler to respond to.

AGE RANGE
2–3 years

LEARNING OPPORTUNITIES

- To increase level of concentration
- To develop memory skills
- To develop vocabulary.

YOU WILL NEED

A large flat tray; ball; toy car; wooden block; teddy; torch; piece of bright fabric; small box; table.

Remember, remember

Sharing the game

- Start the game by placing all the items inside the small box.
- Then take each item out of the box and encourage your child to name it and describe it.
- After all the items have been taken out of the box and named, place them on the table.
- Direct your child to pick up the teddy and put it beside the wooden block.
- Then tell her to choose the ball and to place it next to the car.
- Now ask her to take each item, one by one, and place it on the large tray. Remind her of the name of each item and ask her to repeat the word each time.
- Touch each item and describe where it is in comparison to the other items. Encourage your toddler to join in.
- Next, explain that you are going to cover the items with the fabric.
- Having done this, tell your toddler that you want her to close her eyes while you take an item away.
- While her eyes are closed, slip your hand under the fabric and withdraw one of the items. Put it out of sight.
- Challenge your toddler to guess what is missing from the tray.

Taking it further

- Carry out this game in different rooms. For each room, present your toddler with a selection of items that relate to the particular room. For example, when in the bathroom, use items such as a toothbrush, flannel and plastic duck.

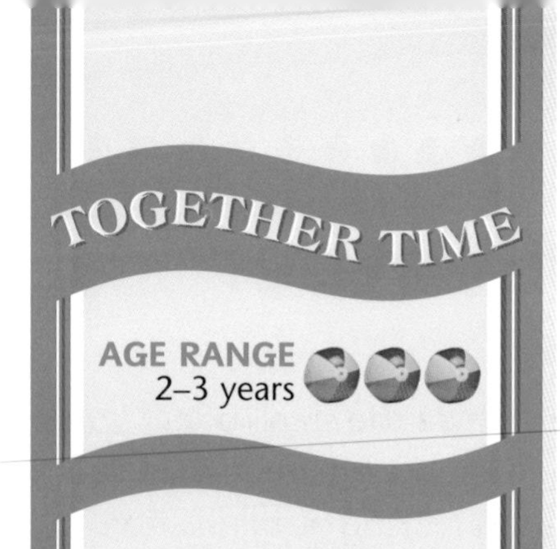

AGE RANGE
2–3 years

LEARNING OPPORTUNITIES
- To encourage vocabulary development
- To develop matching skills
- To develop memory skills.

YOU WILL NEED
A box; belt; bunch of keys; doll; sun-hat; baseball cap; book; necklace; make-up; toy; sock; picture book with family members in it (or pictures from magazines representing family members).

Family box

Sharing the game

- Place the variety of items inside the box.
- Read the book about the family or look at the pictures of a 'mum', 'dad', 'granny', 'auntie', 'uncle', 'brother' and 'sister'. Talk about the pictures, being sensitive to your child's circumstances.
- Now pick the items out of the box, one at a time. Name each item and describe what it is used for.
- Ask your child to choose an item, then invite him to match it to the person he thinks it belongs to.
- Choose the doll and suggest that it belongs to 'dad'. If your child disagrees, choose another 'wrong' option and challenge him again, before presenting him with a possible right answer!
- Now invite him to match another item to a family member.
- Continue to do this with your child until each item is matched with someone in the family.

Taking it further

- Choose a book about a farm. Provide your child with some toys and pictures of where each animal traditionally lives. Encourage him to match the animals to their homes.

AGE RANGE
2–3 years

LEARNING OPPORTUNITIES

- To develop an awareness of the environment
- To develop the use of vocabulary
- To challenge memory skills.

YOU WILL NEED

Photographs of each room in the house or nursery; two items from each room (choose ones that are easily identifiable as belonging to a specific room); basket or box.

What room?

Sharing the game

- Walk around the house or nursery with your child. Stop a few times in each room, drawing her attention to a variety of items. When you stop, bend to her level, so that you are both looking at things from the same viewpoint.
- Come back to your original room and sit with your child. Look at the photographs together. Can she name the room and point anything out?
- Invite your child to choose an item from the box. Challenge her to name it and identify the room that it should be in.
- Continue to do this with each item. Name it, discuss it and match it with the room that it belongs to.

- Make some obviously wrong suggestions, such as asking your child to put the cutlery in the bedroom or the bathroom! Encourage her to tell you that this is wrong and help her to explain why.

Taking it further

- Cut out from a magazine or catalogue items that could be placed in a specific room. Offer your child a glue stick and invite her to choose some of the items to create a kitchen or bedroom picture.

AGE RANGE
2–3 years

LEARNING OPPORTUNITIES

- To develop an awareness of colour
- To encourage the use of matching skills
- To relate colour to self and the environment.

YOU WILL NEED

Three boxes (one red, one blue and one yellow); red, blue and yellow items to put into the boxes; three large pieces of fabric to match the boxes and items; red, blue and yellow T-shirts or jumpers for your child (and you, if possible).

Colour explosion

Sharing the game

- Roll out the large pieces of fabric and place the matching coloured box on to each piece.
- Sit on one of the pieces of fabric with your child and explore the contents of the box with him. Name each item.
- Now move to the other pieces of fabric in turn and repeat the process for each colour.

- Move the boxes to one side and challenge your child to find colour-matching items to place on each piece of fabric.
- Ask your child to pick his favourite three blue items, his favourite three yellow items and his favourite three red items. Put them all in a pile. Name each item that he chooses and talk about its use.
- Now invite him to choose a T-shirt and help him to put it on.
- Encourage him to walk around the house or nursery with you, and gather a few items of the colour that he is wearing. Use the T-shirt to remind him of the colour that he is looking for and try not to prompt him using language.
- Change the colour of his T-shirt and repeat the process. Repeat again for the third colour.
- Add the items that your child finds to the boxes.

Taking it further

- Help your child to make a small display of the items that he has gathered. Place the fabric on a shelf or small table, then put the items on the fabric.

CHAPTER 8

WINDING DOWN

Babies and toddlers spend part of their days being lively. They look for interaction, want to be entertained and enjoy being actively involved in a variety of activities. They also spend a good deal of time resting, enjoying quiet moments and sleeping. It is important that we demonstrate that it is positive to be quiet and calm, and that we set up specific times when activities to support this calmness and quietness are offered. The games in this chapter provide a wealth of suggestions for helping your child to relax and enjoy quiet moments, both alone and together with you.

SLEEP

A new baby can sleep as much as 16 hours a day, sometimes only waking to be fed. It is therefore important to ensure that you have a warm, cosy place for him to be comfortable in. Some experts believe that, during the daytime hours, it is best to let him sleep somewhere different from where you put him down for the night. They think that this helps the baby to begin to distinguish between night and day. However, all babies are different and, as a parent, you will quickly come to know where your child sleeps most comfortably.

Think first! Remember that it is very dangerous to let your baby overheat. It is important that you follow the Government advice for avoiding cot death. Leaflets are available from your health visitor or doctor.

How you can help

- Watch and listen to your baby and learn to identify the signs telling you that he needs to rest or sleep.
- Lie quietly beside him on a soft rug, mat or bed, whisper and sing quietly to relax him.
- Ensure that you place him in a secure, cosy but well-ventilated area or cot.
- Introduce routines before sleep times. For example, you may choose to rock your baby to sleep and then place him gently into the most comfortable sleeping area. Or perhaps you will choose to place him down, gently speaking to him, offering comfort and reassurance. He may drift off to sleep with music playing. You will find what best suits your baby.
- When your baby is waking, allow him to gradually wake up fully, staying close by for reassurance. Welcome him back to his exciting world in his own time.

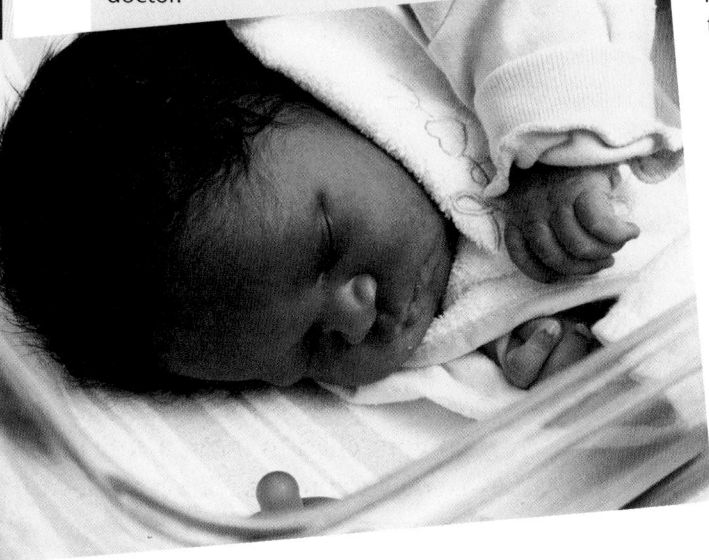

QUIET STIMULATION

By the age of one, your baby is awake for longer periods and is generally only having one main nap per day. Although he is now sleeping less, he still needs rest periods and time to be quiet. If he has time to relax and rest, he is more likely to stay healthy and less likely to become ill. If he is tired, he may become bad-tempered, irritable, lose concentration and not enjoy any activity that he becomes involved in.

How you can help

- Hold your baby, cuddle and stroke him, tickle him gently, close your eyes and pretend to yawn.
- Take your baby in your arms and walk around the room. Draw his attention to ornaments, pictures, a fruit bowl and other objects of interest.
- Place jelly, cooked pasta or instant dessert mix on a tray for him to play with. This has a calming effect.
- Put on some quiet music and slowly dance around the room.
- In his waking moments, provide him with colourful items to look at. Hang kite fabric, linens and cottons above where you sit to feed him. Attach lengths of ribbon for hanging small interesting items for him to look at. Change these items regularly.
- Set up experiences which means that your baby does not have to communicate verbally or concentrate too much.

RELAXATION

Try to involve your child in a quiet, relaxing experience once he has become tired and has lost interest in his usual activities. Something as simple as singing quietly, reading together or playing a 'Copy me' game, can help him to relax, wind down and become ready to settle into his nap.

Routines reassure young children. Introducing routines can help your child to relax after busy, active experiences. Provide interesting, simple and soothing experiences for you both to enjoy together.

After very active periods, try to offer your child some space and the appropriate resources to settle him for relaxation. Take a step back during these quiet moments and let him concentrate and focus himself without interruption. Try not to break his concentration and ensure that you do not over-stimulate him during these times. Never force your young child to be quiet and still. These types of activities should be presented only if they are appropriate. If your child remains busy and does not need to rest, then play games with him, ensuring that you allow him to keep busy until he loses interest.

How you can help

- Don't put out too many things. Offer your child something that he can do himself with ease and without support.
- Activities that encourage him to use his sense of touch can be set up in a quiet and calm atmosphere.
- Spend these times within reach of a comfortable space with cushions and blankets for him, should he want them.
- Place any toy or comforter that he may want nearby.
- Use this quiet time to reflect on what he has been doing – evaluating and encouraging him to recall what he has been involved with.

WINDING DOWN

AGE RANGE
0–1 year

LEARNING OPPORTUNITIES

- To encourage recognition of self
- To encourage focus and attention
- To stimulate visual awareness.

YOU WILL NEED

A large mirror (fixed if possible); damp cloth; dry cloth; baby lotion; icing sugar in a tube; teddy; toy car.

Mirror faces

Sharing the game

- Lead your child to the mirror in whichever way is appropriate. For example, you may take him by the hand, encourage him to pad along by supporting him under the arms, or you may invite him to crawl by crawling with him.
- Place your baby on your knee or sit him between your legs and face the mirror together.

- Talk into the mirror to your baby, pointing out his reflection. Draw his attention to his features.
- Sketch a simple face on the mirror with the tube of icing sugar. Show your baby the eyes that you have drawn, then gently touch his face beside his eye, repeating the word 'eye'.
- Pick up the teddy and make him dance, encouraging your baby to watch the teddy's reflection in the mirror. Let your baby hold the teddy while you draw a simple teddy shape with the icing sugar on the mirror.
- Next, take the car and run it along the length of your baby's legs and the floor. Make car noises as you do this.
- Take the icing sugar, while continuing to make an engine noise, and draw the shape of a car. While you draw, say, 'Will it be a face? Will it be a teddy? No, it's a car!'.

Taking it further

- Smudge baby lotion over the mirror so that your baby's face disappears. Bit by bit, wipe off the lotion to see your baby's hair, eyes, nose, mouth and chin.

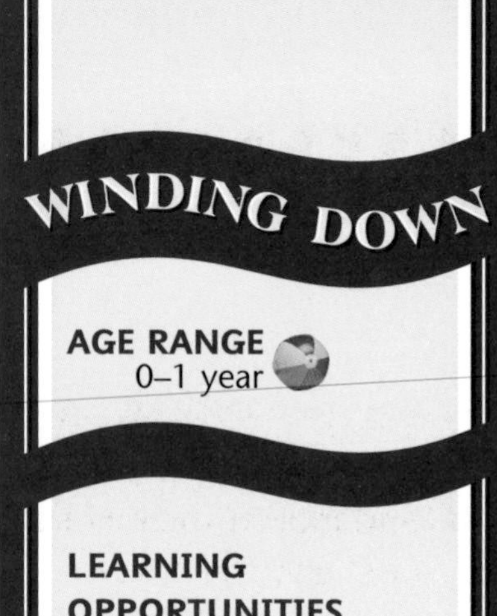

AGE RANGE
0–1 year

LEARNING OPPORTUNITIES
- To introduce contrasting colours
- To stimulate listening skills
- To encourage visual awareness.

YOU WILL NEED
White and yellow card; felt-tipped pens; saucer; bowl; dinner plate; ribbon; laminator or sticky-backed plastic; scissors.

Compare and contrast

Sharing the game

- Draw around the bowl on to the card six times to create six circles. Cut them out.
- Repeat this with the saucer and then the dinner plate. Make sure that some of the discs are yellow and some are white.
- Use the felt-tipped pens to draw bold patterns on to the discs. Stripes, zigzags, swirls, criss-crosses and dots create interesting patterns. Use a pen colour that contrasts with the colour of the card.
- Laminate each disc or cover it with sticky-backed plastic.
- Sit with your baby on the floor and present each disc to her. Talk about the patterns while you trace them with your fingers.
- Attach ribbon to the discs and hang them securely beside your baby's bouncy chair or above the changing mat.

Taking it further

- Create similar sets of other shapes, such as squares or hexagons. Use star shapes, circles and flowers to create the patterns.
- Create a black set of discs and use holographic paper to make interesting patterns on them.
- Use material such as fur, felt, and rough linen to create shapes on a set of the discs. Encourage your baby to feel and trace the textures that are on the discs.

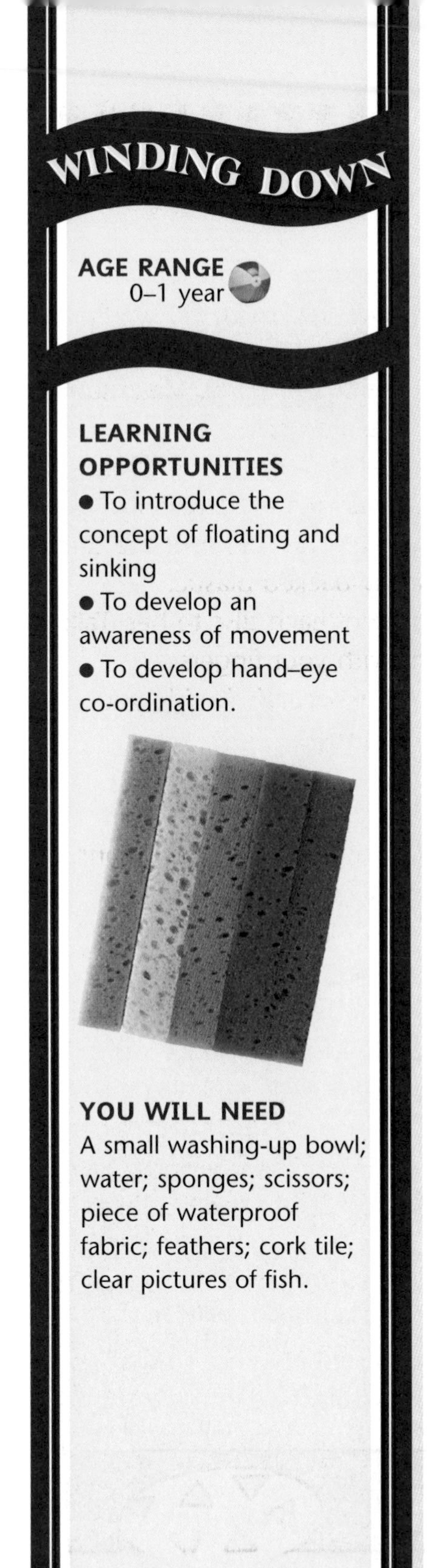

WINDING DOWN

AGE RANGE
0–1 year

LEARNING OPPORTUNITIES
- To introduce the concept of floating and sinking
- To develop an awareness of movement
- To develop hand–eye co-ordination.

YOU WILL NEED
A small washing-up bowl; water; sponges; scissors; piece of waterproof fabric; feathers; cork tile; clear pictures of fish.

Watch the fish

Sharing the game

- Cut small and large fish shapes out of the sponges, fabric and cork tile. Find some feathers that can be shaped into small fish shapes.
- Sit on the floor with your baby beside you and look at the pictures of the fish together. Point out the 'tail', the 'nose' and the 'fin'.
- Pretend to make fish noises, placing your lips against your baby's palm as you make the shapes and noises with your mouth.
- Sit with your baby next to the bowl of water.
- Use your hands to 'swim' through the water in the bowl. Tell your baby that you are pretending to be a fish!
- Take one of the cut-out fish and place it into the water. Encourage your baby to help the 'fish' swim around the bowl.
- Invite him to pop some other fish into the bowl and to play with them.
- Sink each cork fish to the bottom and allow it to pop back up so that your baby watches the first movement.
- Gently blow the fish to move them around the bowl.

Taking it further

- Lift out one of the sponge fish from the bowl and squeeze the water out of it. Show your baby what you are doing. Let him feel the water dripping out.

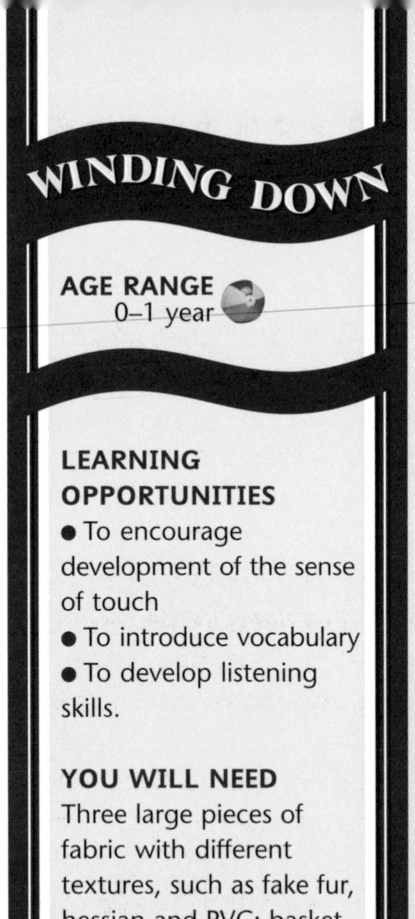

WINDING DOWN

AGE RANGE 0–1 year

LEARNING OPPORTUNITIES
- To encourage development of the sense of touch
- To introduce vocabulary
- To develop listening skills.

YOU WILL NEED
Three large pieces of fabric with different textures, such as fake fur, hessian and PVC; basket or box; small textured items such as felt, sponge, a fir cone, a piece of cork, and a comb.

Match the feel

Sharing the game

- Roll out the fur fabric and encourage your baby to roll on it, lie on it and rub her feet and hands on it.
- Sit on the floor with her, using the edges of the fabric to tickle her.
- Take a piece of felt, natural sponge and silk handkerchief. Offer them to your baby, watching her closely. Use them to tickle her, then place them on the fur.
- Take the hessian fabric and place it next to the fur. Crawl on to it. Run your hand over the fur saying, 'Soft, soft, soft', then over the hessian, saying, 'Rough, rough, rough'.

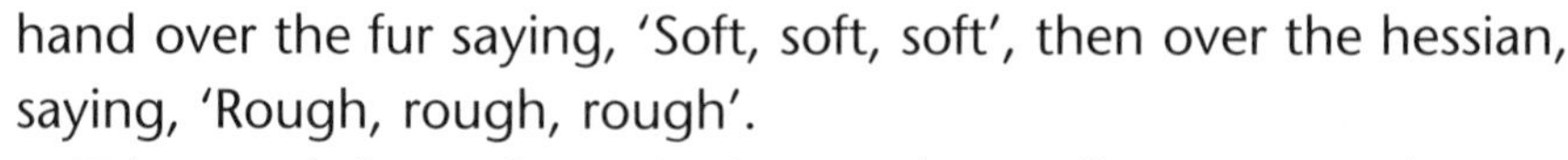

- Take rough items from the box such as a fir cone, pumice stone and piece of bark, and let your baby explore them, repeating the word 'rough'.
- Next, roll out the PVC fabric. Place items from the box such as a comb, a piece of Duplo and a wellington boot on to the fabric for your baby to touch and examine.
- Explore the items with your baby and use appropriate language to describe the textures.
- Ensure that you are always nearby, closely supervising, so that your baby feels safe. Gently persuade her not to put items into her mouth.

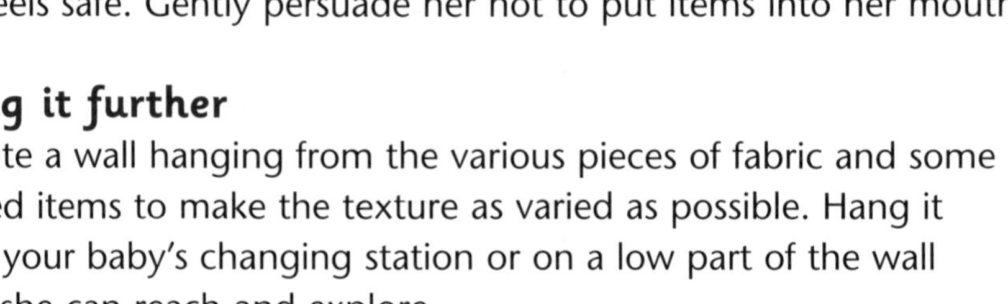

Taking it further

- Create a wall hanging from the various pieces of fabric and some textured items to make the texture as varied as possible. Hang it beside your baby's changing station or on a low part of the wall where she can reach and explore.

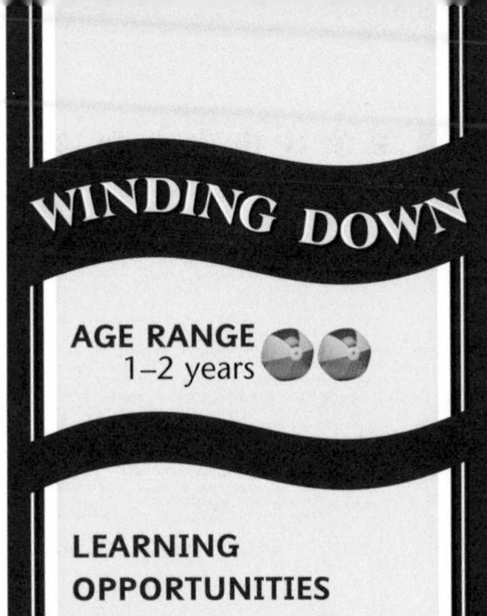

AGE RANGE
1–2 years

LEARNING OPPORTUNITIES
- To stimulate the visual senses
- To encourage an environmental awareness
- To encourage relaxation.

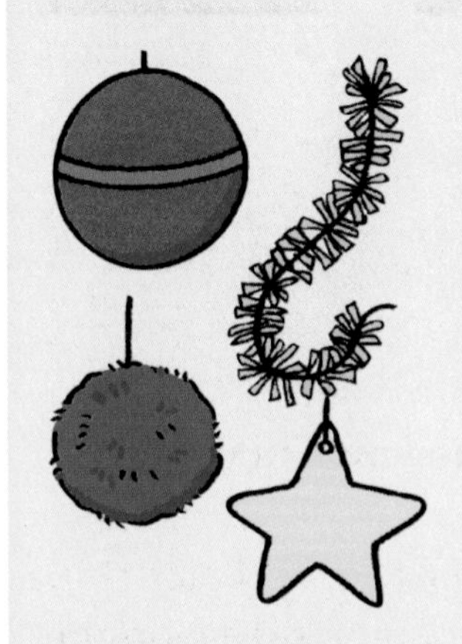

YOU WILL NEED
A comfortable space; large cushions or pillows; lengths of dark blue fabric; ribbon or string; sticky tape; selection of interesting objects such as tinsel, pompoms, sequins, glowing stars and planets; box or bag.

Under the stars

Sharing the game

- Prepare a comfortable area by hanging the fabric. Drape it from the ceiling or across a corner, attempting to create a canopy to hang the various items from.
- Place all the interesting items into the box or bag and invite your toddler to sit or lie with you under the 'sky'.
- Offer the bag or box to your toddler and allow him to explore its contents. Name the items for him as he gives his attention to each.
- Ask your toddler to choose an item for you to hang in the 'sky'. (He might not want you to take them away, so, if possible, have more than one of each item so that you can hang one and leave him the other to explore.)
- Encourage your toddler to choose a few other items to hang. Each time, describe and name the item for him before fixing it to the sky with string and sticky tape.
- Once you have hung a few items, stop and suggest that you both sit or lie down again to look at the 'sky'. Talk about how it has changed.
- Continue the game for as long as your toddler wishes.

Taking it further

- Hang some green and blue fabric and some strawberry netting, and create an underwater world.
- Paint a rainbow on to a piece of paper to attach to some blue fabric, then hang coloured items (in rainbow colours) for your toddler to watch while he rests.

AGE RANGE
1–2 years

LEARNING OPPORTUNITIES
- To encourage listening and responding
- To relate action to words
- To encourage use of language through singing.

YOU WILL NEED
Four or five favourite songs; coloured pens; paper; brightly-coloured ring binder. Draw a picture on the paper or trace an appropriate picture from a colouring book that will represent the main character or object from each song, for example, a farmer for 'Old Macdonald Had a Farm' (Traditional). Place each song and the picture the ring binder.

Simple songs

Sharing the game

- Sit with your toddler and sing one of your chosen familiar songs.
- Open the ring binder and let her look through it until she finds the picture to match the song.
- Sing the song again, using body language, movements and facial expressions to accompany it. For example:

Twinkle, twinkle little star
(waggle the fingers of both hands in front of you)
How I wonder what you are;
(place both hands on cheeks and look to the sky)
Up above the world so high
(move your hands above your head, still waggling the fingers)
Like a diamond in the sky;
(change your fingers to make a diamond shape)
Twinkle, twinkle little star
(waggle the fingers of both hands in front of you)
How I wonder what you are.
(place both hands on cheeks and look to the sky)

- Repeat the process with the other songs in your binder.

Taking it further

- Each time you sing another song, make a page for the book and think of simple actions to support the message of the words.

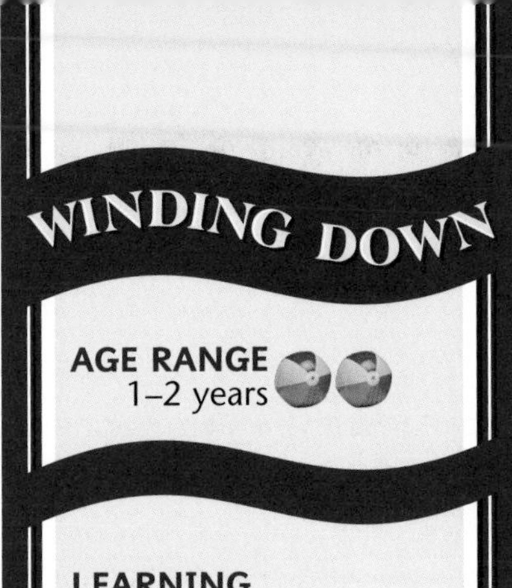

LEARNING OPPORTUNITIES

- To encourage appreciation of art
- To introduce works of art
- To encourage creative response.

YOU WILL NEED

Five or six art prints such as *Sunflowers* by Van Gogh and *Water Lilies* by Monet (try to have five or six very different kinds); laminator or sticky-backed plastic; Blu-Tack; pastels or crayons; paper.

The art world

Sharing the game

- Either laminate your chosen art prints or cover them with sticky-backed plastic.
- Sit with your toddler and show him the art prints. Talk about what you can see together, encouraging him to use any words that he knows, such as 'flower', 'pretty' and so on.
- Look in detail at one of the pictures. For example, discuss the number of flowers and their colour, talk about whether the colours used are bright or dull, and so on.
- Now let your toddler look at all the prints together. Ask him which one he likes the most. Let him choose one to pick up and look at.
- Invite your toddler to help you to choose where to hang the pictures. You might suggest somewhere in his room, or near to where he eats or sits to play. Let him carry the pictures to the right place.
- Whenever you are near to a picture, draw his attention to it. Point out new things each time, as well as his favourite parts of the picture.
- Change the prints for a different set on a regular basis.

Taking it further

- Use the laminated art prints as place mats. Talk about the pictures during meal times.
- Give your toddler some pastels or crayons (in the same shades as one of the prints). Invite him to use the print as an inspiration to create his own work of art!

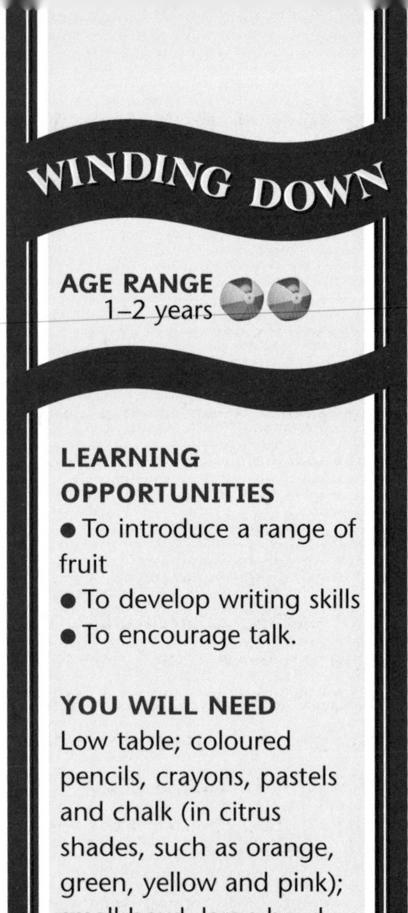

WINDING DOWN

AGE RANGE
1–2 years

LEARNING OPPORTUNITIES

- To introduce a range of fruit
- To develop writing skills
- To encourage talk.

YOU WILL NEED

Low table; coloured pencils, crayons, pastels and chalk (in citrus shades, such as orange, green, yellow and pink); small bowl; large bowl; two limes; two lemons; two oranges; scissors; white paper discs.

Fruit bowl

Sharing the game

- Place the full bowl of fruit on the low table and invite your toddler to explore the fruit.
- Encourage her to name the different fruit, identifying the colour and feel of each.
- Invite your toddler to smell it and offer it to her to taste – hopefully she will say 'no'! If she does not, then just before she tastes it, exclaim that you were rather silly and that you must cut it first!

- Cut one of each fruit and offer it to her to smell and taste. Try it with her, describing it as you taste and smell it.
- Place your selection of mark-makers in a small bowl. Offer these and the discs of paper to your toddler.
- Take a disc of paper yourself and pick up a piece of fruit. Choose a mark-maker of that colour and draw the shape of the fruit on to the paper. Colour in the shape.
- Make sure that your child can see what you are doing, and hopefully she will try to copy you.
- Repeat the process with a different-coloured fruit and encourage your child to copy what you are doing.

Taking it further

- Repeat this activity with exotic fruit, vegetables and flowers.
- Display your toddler's pictures in a simple clip frame. Hang it up in the house, perhaps near to the fruit bowl or in the kitchen. Make sure that your toddler sees it too.

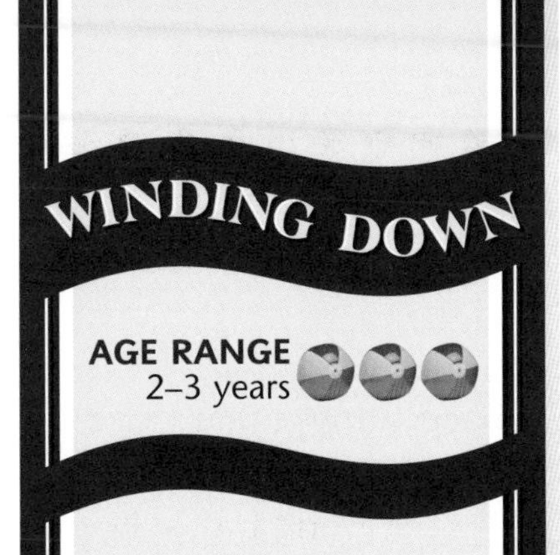

AGE RANGE
2–3 years

LEARNING OPPORTUNITIES
- To encourage quiet restfulness
- To encourage exploration
- To develop an enjoyment of being quiet and still.

YOU WILL NEED
An empty space; fabrics; pillows; cushions; large basket; natural items such as a wooden pot, a large feather and fir cones; box; clean swing bin; scarves; hats; items of clothing.

Calm corner

Sharing the game

- Invite your child to help you to create a little 'oasis' for him to rummage in.
- Suggest that you clear an area in his room with his help. Then ask him to help you put some different-textured cushions and pillows in the area (you can create textured cushions and pillows by wrapping items of clothing such as jumpers and skirts around them).
- Make up a basket of natural items such as a wooden spoon, a small metal pot, a piece of leather, a large feather, fir cones, a natural sponge and so on. Place the basket next to the pillows in your child's 'oasis'.
- Make a backdrop and canopy to the area by draping and attaching fabrics to the ceiling and corners of the area. Try to make a textured wall with a selection of fabrics, and perhaps a 'door' that can be tied back. Offer your child some fabrics to choose from and let him help you to decorate the area.
- Now give your child the box and encourage him to use it to gather some of his favourite toys in. Invite him to bring the box of toys into the space.
- Fill the swing bin with pieces of fabric, scarves, hats and clothing for him to explore. Place the swing bin in a corner of the space.

Taking it further

- Play some calming music while your child is exploring the contents of the boxes.
- Create a set of pictures for your child to look at and talk about (such as photographs, pictures cut from magazines, comics or simple drawings). Place them in another box in the area.

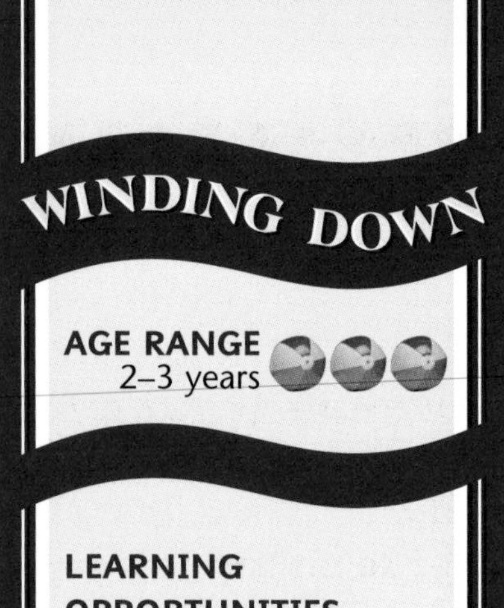

AGE RANGE
2–3 years

LEARNING OPPORTUNITIES

- To encourage sharing and turn-taking
- To encourage sharing of feelings
- To develop an awareness of emotions.

YOU WILL NEED

A story about being happy, such as *I'm Happy* by Karen Bryant-Mole (Hodder Wayland); lolly sticks; straws; felt-tipped pens; crayons; sticky tape; paper discs. Draw simple expressions on to some of the discs, such as a happy face, a sad face and an angry face.

Pass the smile

Sharing the game

- Ask your child what makes her happy. Suggest things that make you happy, such as eating ice-cream, being tickled, playing chase and so on.
- Read the story and talk about it as you look at each page. When a character in the story feels happy, make happy expressions and encourage your child to join in, too.
- When the story is finished, hold up your little expression discs and ask your child to guess what each one is. Choose the happy one and as you hold it say, 'I feel happy'.
- Give the disc to your child and encourage her to say it too.
- Repeat the game with each disc.
- Vary the game by showing that you are happy, for example, by giving a hug or a handshake.

Taking it further

- Put pens and crayons on a low table. Offer your child a disc and explain that she may create a face on it. Before she starts, ask her what expression she is going to draw. Write the appropriate word on the back of the disc, then let her create her own 'happy' disc to share. Help her to attach a stick or straw to create a handle.

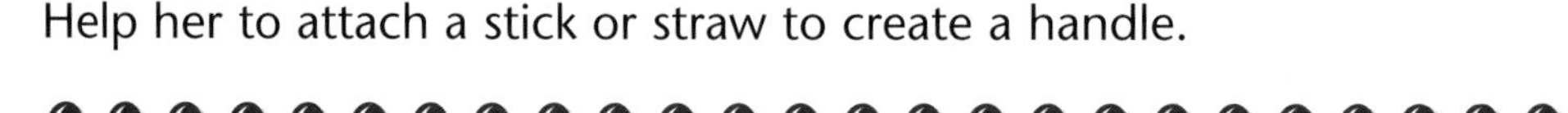

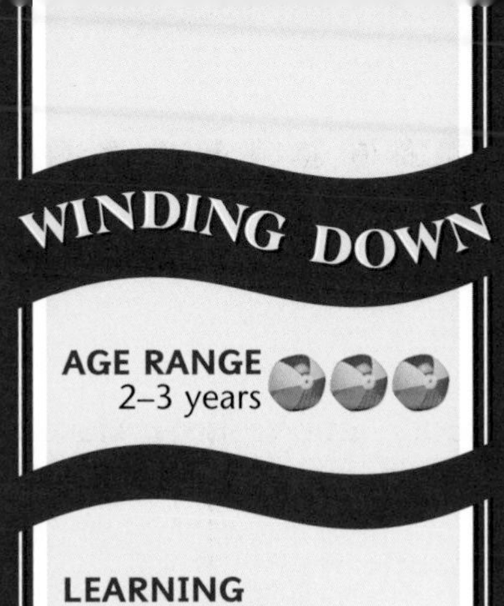

AGE RANGE
2–3 years

LEARNING OPPORTUNITIES
- To encourage manipulation
- To develop an awareness of change
- To develop an appreciation of colour.

YOU WILL NEED
Low table; large tray with sides; apron; bottle of baby oil or sunflower oil; food colourings or paints; small squeezable bottles (useful but not essential); paper; newspaper.

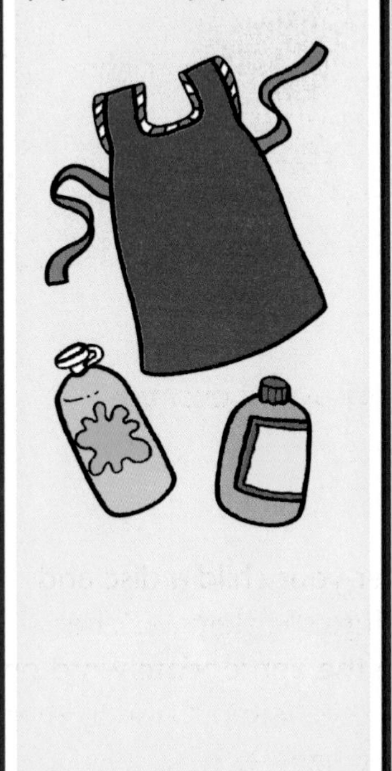

Oil painting

Sharing the game

- Show each of the items to your child and name it as you ask him to place it on the table.
- Help your child to put his apron on.
- Invite him to squirt or pour some of the oil into the tray. You will need enough to cover the bottom of the tray.
- Ask your child to pick up the tray and gently tip it so that the oil spreads evenly over the bottom.
- Next, encourage him to choose a colour of paint or food colouring and to drip four or five drops of colour into the oil. Count the drops with him.
- Invite your child to tip the tray backwards and forwards, and to watch the colour and oil drops move but not mix. Ask him to use his fingers to mix the oil and colour. (Note that it will not mix properly).
- Try to do the mixing together and let your child enjoy the relaxing and therapeutic effect of manipulating the mixture.

Taking it further

- Ask your child to add another colour to the tray. Let him manipulate the mixture by tipping the tray and by using his fingers and perhaps a spoon. Then invite him to place a piece of paper gently on to the mixture. Lift it out carefully for him and place the print on a sheet of newspaper to let it dry.

WINDING DOWN

AGE RANGE
2–3 years

LEARNING OPPORTUNITIES

- To encourage an understanding of imitation
- To encourage role-play
- To develop imagination.

YOU WILL NEED

A story about robots (a simple, made-up one is ideal); two hats; two pairs of sun-glasses; two plastic cups; two tissues; bin; box.

Robots

Sharing the game

- Sit quietly with your child and tell her a story about robots. Make it short and simple, repeating parts so that she can remember it. Alternatively, read a story about robots, talking about what happens on each page and drawing your child's attention to the pictures.
- Now suggest that you play 'Robots'. Explain that this means that you will do something and that your child must copy your action.
- Sit opposite each other and begin. Do some simple things such as tapping your head, covering your eyes and turning your head slowly from side to side.
- If your child is enjoying this and joining in, start to move a little more. For example, you could stand up then sit down again; stand and turn around; walk like a robot, and so on.
- Move back to the sitting area with your child. Put the props into the box and introduce it to the game. Choose a hat and put it on, then the glasses. Next, choose a tissue and pretend to blow your nose. Stand and walk to the bin, placing your tissue in it.
- Now invite your child to take the lead.

Taking it further

- Introduce a voice for your robot. Before carrying out an action or movement, explain in your robot voice what you are going to do.
- Ask your child questions using your robot voice, encouraging her to create a robot voice of her own.

RHYMES AND VERSES

Here are some verses to share with your young child. The more you talk to him, the more he will respond. The verses that you say don't need to make sense or even to rhyme, but if possible, they should relate to what you are asking him to participate in.

Good morning!

Hello, hello
How are you today?
Hello, hello
Hip, hip, hip hooray.
The grass is green
The sky is blue
The birds do sweetly sing
Oh, oh, oh, happy day. Happy day!

Alice Sharp

Bouncing treat

Shiny, shimmering,
silver ball,
reach and touch it
make it fall.

Coloured ribbons,
green and red,
standing straight
they touch your head.

Alice Sharp

Exercise, exercise

Stretch up high
Then down low
Touch your head
Then your toe.

Reach out wide
Fold right in
Big and round
Small and thin.

Alice Sharp

Walk here and there

Walk through puddles
On your toes
Lift a flower
Up to your nose.

Feel the grass
Beneath your feet
Pile up leaves
Beside your seat.

Alice Sharp

Enjoying the weather

The sun has got his hat on hip, hip, hip hooray.
The sun has got his hat on and we're going out to play.

The rain is falling slowly, drip, drip, drip today.
The rain is falling slowly and we can't go out to play.

The wind is blowing wildly, cold and blustery.
The wind is blowing wildly and we're staying in today.

And now the snow is falling, softly to the ground.
Softly, softly falling, and making not one sound.

Squeeze and stretch

Soft and squidgy
Gooey too
Pull and stretch it
Taste it too.

On your fingers
On your nose
Drip and rub
It on your toes.

Alice Sharp

TRADITIONAL RHYMES

Use these traditional rhymes to increase your child's vocabulary and to introduce her to aspects of the world around her.

Do Your Ears Hang Low?

Do your ears hang low?
Do they wobble to and fro?
Can you tie them in a knot?
Can you tie them in a bow?
Can you fling them over your shoulder,
Like a regimental soldier?
Do your ears hang low?

Traditional

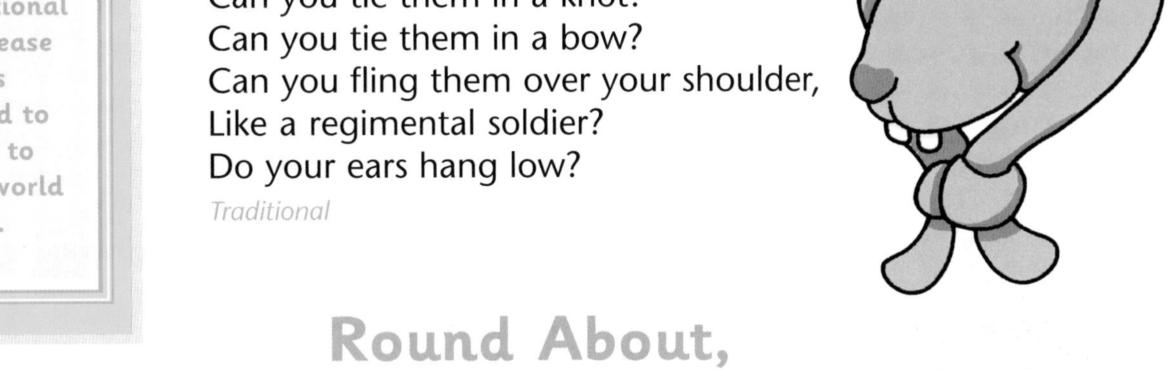

Round About, Round About

Round about, round about
Runs the wee mouse.
Up a step, up a step
In his wee house.

Traditional

USING THE RHYME

Your child will enjoy sharing this closely with you. Hold his hand in yours and run your fingers around his palm, then up and under his chin.

Row, Row, Row Your Boat

Row, row, row your boat,
Gently down the stream;
Merrily, merrily, merrily, merrily,
Life is but a dream.

Rock, rock, rock your boat,
Gently to and fro;
Merrily, merrily, merrily, merrily,
Down the stream we go!

Row, row, row your boat,
Gently down the stream;
If you see a crocodile,
Don't forget to scream!

Traditional

USING THE RHYME

This will encourage your child to move in time to the rhyme with you.

Two Little Eyes

Two little eyes to look all around,
Two little ears to hear any sound;
One little nose to smell what's sweet,
One little mouth that likes to eat.

Traditional

RECOMMENDED BOOKS

Present your child with regular opportunities to listen and respond to story-books and picture books. This will encourage a close relationship and offer a time for quiet moments.

- *I'm Happy, I'm Bored, I'm Shy, I'm Worried, I'm Special, I'm Lonely* and *It's not fair* (all published by Wayland). A useful series of books about different emotions. They can all be used for sharing with your child during a quiet time and for 'winding down'.

- *Twinkle Twinkle Little Star, The Wheels on the Bus, Cosy Cat, Whose Bottom?* and *Whose Ears?*, all by M Butterfield (Ladybird). A range of board books to share with your child. They encourage plenty of active involvement.

- The *Mr Men* and *Little Miss* series of books, including *Mr Tickle, Mr Happy, Mr Nosey, Mr Funny, Mr Greedy, Mr Bump, Little Miss Giggles* and *Little Miss Bossy*, all by Roger Hargreaves (World International Ltd). Many of these can be supported with visual aids, as most of them have a character toy to go with them. The use of such props will help even the youngest of children feel involved in the story.

- *My Mum is Fantastic, My Dad is Brilliant, My Grandpa is Amazing* and *My Grandma is Wonderful*, all by Nick Butterworth (Walker Books). This series of books helps to highlight the importance of family. The illustrations are exciting and can be used to stimulate endless discussion, providing plenty of giggles!

- *I Want to Be* and *I Want my Potty*, both by Tony Ross (Collins Picture Lions). Two books to encourage young children's awareness of themselves.

- *Whose House?, Whose Feet?, Whose Ears?* and *Whose Nose?*, all by Jeannette Rowe (Southwood Books). A set of lift-the-flap books, that will draw your child into the pictures.

- *Ollie's Weather, Ollie's Colours, Ollie's Opposites* and *Ollie's 1, 2, 3*, all by Tim Warnes (Walker Books). A set of informative books published for the Early Learning Centre.

- *Bertie and Small's Fast Bike Ride* and *Bertie and Small's Brave Sea Journey*, both by Vanessa Cabban (Walker Books)

- *Scruffy Teddy Looks for a Friend, Scruffy Teddy Loses His Sock, Scruffy Teddy Plays Hide and Seek* and *Scruffy Teddy and the Lost Ball*, all by Gaynor Berry (Parragon Books)

- *The Biggest Bed in the World* by Lindsay Camp (Harper Collins)

- *Count Down to Bedtime* by Mike Haines (Hodder Children's Books)

- *Life with Loopy* by Libby Butterworth (Picture Lions)

- *Dear Zoo* by Rod Campbell (Puffin)

- *Mog and Barnaby, Mog and Bunny, Mog in the Dark* and *Mog and the Baby*, all by Judith Kerr (Picture Lions)

- The *Maisy* series of books by Lucy Cousins (Walker Books)

- *Molly at the Dentist* by Angie Sage (David and Charles Children's Books)

- *Peekaboo Baby* by Mandy Ross (Ladybird)

- The *Kipper* series of books by Mick Inkpen (Hodder Children's Books)

- *The Wibbly Pig* series of books by Mick Inkpen (Hodder Children's Books)